PROJECT MANAGEMENT
MADE SIMPLE

PROJECT MANAGEMENT MADE SIMPLE

A Guide to Successful Management of Computer Systems Projects

David King

YOURDON Press
P T R Prentice Hall
Englewood Cliffs, New Jersey 07632

Library of Congress Cataloging-in-Publication Data

King, David,
    Project management made simple : a guide to successful management
of computer systems projects / David King.
        p.   cm. -- (Yourdon Press computing series)
    Includes bibliographical references and index.
    ISBN 0-13-717729-1
    1. Industrial project management.   I. Title. II. Series.
T56.8.K49 1992
658.4'04--dc20   91-13660
                                                       CIP

Editorial/production supervision: Mary P. Rottino
Cover design: Bruce Kenselaar
Manufacturing buyer: Susan Brunke
Prepress buyer: Mary Elizabeth McCartney
Acquisitions editor: Paul W. Becker
Editorial assistant: Noreen Regina

The publisher offers discounts on this book when ordered
in bulk quantities. For more information, write:

> Special Sales/Professional Marketing
> Prentice Hall
> Professional & Technical Reference Division
> Englewood Cliffs, New Jersey 07632

Printed in the United States of America
10 9 8 7 6

ISBN 0-13-717729-1

Prentice-Hall International (UK) Limited, *London*
Prentice-Hall of Australia Pty. Limited, *Sydney*
Prentice-Hall Canada Inc., *Toronto*
Prentice-Hall Hispanoamericana, S.A., *Mexico*
Prentice-Hall of India Private Limited, *New Delhi*
Prentice-Hall of Japan, Inc., *Tokyo*
Simon & Schuster Asia Pte. Ltd., *Singapore*
Editora Prentice-Hall do Brasil, *Rio de Janeiro*

For Gloria

CONTENTS

- *Pre-packaged software*
- *Systems developed using Fourth Generation Languagess (4GLs) and Application Generators etc.*
- *Systems developed using Object-Oriented techniques*
- *Prototyped applications*
- *Systems developed with no life cycle techniques at all*

8: The Future of Project Management   **103**

What Project Management techniques and procedures will be required in the future? This chapter is a direct extrapolation of the previous chapter and attempts to predict some of the changes that could affect the discipline of project management

References   **107**

Index   **109**

PREFACE

It is no better to accept without verification the word of a computer than the word of another mathematician. In fact the tedium of routine tasks makes programming errors extremely probable. We cannot possibly achieve what I regard as the essential element of a proof—our own personal understanding—if part of the argument is hidden away in a box.

F. F. Bonsall, *A Down-to-Earth View of Mathematics*, American Mathematical Monthly, No. 89 (1982), p. 13. (MacMillan Education, Ltd., Basingstoke, England.)

Project management is a discipline that is given much lip service in the computer systems industry but is not always heeded in the heat of systems development battles. Many volumes of text and diagrams have been devoted to project management and, recently, many software packages have been deployed to help automate the various tasks of the project manager. Nevertheless, systems development projects still suffer from a lack of proper project management, leading to painful surprises in terms of missed schedules, massive budget overruns, inadequate system performance, and (more often than acceptable) the delivery of incomplete functionality.

Why is this? I believe one reason is that all the project management texts and many of the relevant software packages are somewhat unwieldy. Some project management manuals that I have seen are so large that they occupy several feet of book shelf. Also, many project management software packages require a full-time person on the project simply to enter and keep up to date the required information. No wonder project management is a shunned discipline.

Therefore, what I have tried to do in this little book is to provide the practicing and potential systems development project manager with a project management "cook book." I have distilled all the useful project management techniques and information that I have learned into a practical and concise set of recommendations and checklists that can be used as a daily reference manual.

Consequently, this book is not a full-scale compendium of project management techniques and practices, nor is it a detailed exposition of any one project management methodology. It is intended to serve as a sort of "data dictionary" to the vast database of project management information available and, as mentioned, as a daily reference manual to help the project manager through the many and sundry tasks of managing a software development project. But it is only my view at this particular time; as such, it should be added to as the user becomes more experienced and knowledgeable in this rapidly growing field.

I believe that this book will not only be useful to the project manager, but will prove of value to other members of system development teams, including the long-suffering users of the systems. Additionally, executive and corporate management will find this book useful in promoting the understanding and implementation of good project management practices.

ACKNOWLEDGMENTS

My colleagues and friends throughout my life and career have added substantially to my knowledge and understanding of life itself and consequently, among many other contributions, to my appreciation of the need for such a thing as Project Management. Some of the more outstanding contributors to my dabbling in this subject include Ted Hall of IBM and Simpact Systems, David Katch of AGS, Colin Bentley of British Petroleum, and John Singleton of Security Pacific. In addition, I've learned a great deal from all of the organizations that I've worked for and with, notably IBM and Citicorp.

My heartfelt thanks and appreciation to all those people and enterprises and also to all of the long-suffering participants in the seminars, classes, and lectures on Project Management that I have presented over the years. They have all helped to build my beliefs and understanding of a much-maligned yet increasingly important discipline.

1

WHAT IS PROJECT MANAGEMENT?

Man is still the most extraordinary computer of all.

John Fitzgerald Kennedy, May 21, 1963

Those of us who've seen many application software development projects go by may consider that the phrase "Project Management" in this context, is an oxymoron, like "military intelligence," or "political integrity." The success of a system development project will often depend on the length of the project, the amount of excess resources available, how powerful the user is, or from what country or state the hardware, software, or programmers originate. Rarely does success have much to do with the quality of the software produced or the final delivery schedule and costs. Why is this?

I believe it's because many of these projects are not managed properly or at all. It is often been said that we can only manage things that can be measured. Therefore, if we cannot measure what we create, subjective and indirect factors often determine the success or failure of the endeavor. Accordingly, to manage these activities effectively, we need to set up an environment where we can accurately measure and constantly monitor the efforts against a predetermined set of standards and values. Then we can manage! Certainly, not all software development failures could have been avoided by attention to correct project management, but it surely could have helped.

1.1 WHAT DO WE MEAN BY A SOFTWARE DEVELOPMENT PROJECT?

When developing a piece of software, whether for an application system, one or more programs which will form part of a system, or a suite of operating systems modules, a number of activities need to be carried out. In each case, the exact set of activities may vary by a small or large amount. But the one common characteristic should be that there is a start and an end to each set of activities.

A software development *project* is a set of activities that starts and ends at identifiable points in time and that produces quantifiable and qualifiable software deliverables. Along the way, other deliverables will be produced, many in the form of human- and machine-readable documentation. These interim deliverables help to monitor progress of the project, and some of them will form permanent components of the total software package.

So, developing the first deliverable version of an application system for a customer or user is a project. Making a set of specific changes to an existing application system or operating system can also be defined as a project.

The ongoing maintenance of an application system can be defined as a project, as per the foregoing definition, only if it is broken down into time-based "chunks" of work: a year's maintenance and upgrades of system A, for example. Supporting a particular user group's software, however, is not a project with a defined start and end date; it usually continues indefinitely. Also, any one software system or application can be considered to live indefinitely. As soon as a system is installed, the first and all subsequent sets of changes are on their way and will continue indefinitely.

Not all projects are the same. Each will be at least a little different from all other projects. So, to develop a set of rules for project management, we must realize that these rules must be adaptable for all types of projects and, more importantly perhaps, for all types of system developers and system development groups. Additionally, different system development techniques will sometimes require different sets of rules for managing the resulting development activities. For example, a personal computer application developed by using a full-blown application generator will in general require less detailed management control than an application system written in C to run on a large IBM mainframe computer. These variations in rules are discussed more fully in Chapter 7.

1.2 WHY PROJECTS FAIL

As we have all seen, many system development projects fail, as measured by one criterion or another. I define a project as having failed if it fails to meet the user's minimum requirements, *or* is implemented too late to be effective, *or* exceeds its development or operational budget by an unacceptable amount.

There are sometimes purely political reasons for project failures, and these are usually the most unpredictable and least preventable. Nevertheless, for these and other reasons, software projects do fail. Let's examine some of the reasons why this happens so often.

Some *preventable* reasons for project failure include the following:

1. Lack of clear, understandable specifications
2. Poor documentation
3. Poor communications
4. Overambitious objectives
5. Low quality, poor performance
6. Never-ending development
7. High costs and cost overruns
8. Perpetual maintenance

Taking each of these reasons in turn, let's explore them a little further.

1.2.1 Lack of Clear, Understandable Specifications

If the specifications or requirements, in user's terms, are not clear and understandable or do not even exist, the poor system developer has little chance to develop a system that meets the user's needs. This is true even if the developer *is* the user. Often, if not always in this situation, the system *never* becomes fully satisfactory to the user because the user *never* fully defines what the specifications are. In addition to extreme user and developer dissatisfaction, this leads directly to systems that suffer from the "never-ending development" and "perpetual maintenance" syndromes, with the developers continually trying, in vain, to meet the apparently never-ending user's requirements, both before and after implementation.

Even in today's world of object-oriented development, CASE (Computer-Aided Systems Engineering), prototyping, fourth-generation languages (4GLs), and application generators, a clear specification is necessary. In fact, with these modern system development tools, there is even less excuse than before to omit good specifications, because many of the tools themselves provide easy mechanized procedures for creating system and program specifications.

Also, don't fall into the trap of believing that because of the state of the art development tools, written requirements and specifications are not necessary. Without specifications, how will you know what the system is supposed to do? It is like telling your local friendly car salesman to deliver whatever *he'd* like! (Believe me, you *will* get what *he* likes!)

So, if you are responsible for the development of a new system, *insist* on clear specifications from the user and ensure that you and your key development staff understand *all* details of these specifications. To achieve this level of understanding, it is usually necessary to insist on two separate, but related, documents: the user requirements document and the system specification. The latter will be a restatement, in systems professionals' terms, of the user requirements and will demonstrate the developers' understanding, or not, of those requirements. Also, insist that the users stay involved throughout *all* the subsequent stages of system development to ensure that their requirements continue to be met.

1.2.2 Poor Documentation

This problem is akin to the first one of lack of adequate specifications. Most of the deliverables throughout the system development life cycle are composed of documentation. In the "bad old days," this documentation consisted of mountains of paper containing many "Victorian novel" types of documents (terminology courtesy of Tom De Marco), which nobody took (or had) the time to read. So, naturally, as the documentation was not used, it was literally useless. With the advent of structured analysis, design, and programming, and with the introduction of a controlled development life cycle (see reference 1), the production of the required documentary deliverables became much more streamlined, as did the documents themselves. The system design and program documentation have become, in well-managed system development organizations, part of the design and programming processes. This trend has the tremendous advantage of creating documentation that is actually current with the programs themselves, and with the correct management disciplines applied, it is updated along with the programs.

We have not yet reached the programming nirvana, the stage of "self-documenting" programs, which early advocates of COBOL dreamed of, but we are definitely in much better shape now (in the 1990s) in terms of system documentation than we were in the 1960s. This should not lull us into any false sense of security. Good, comprehensive, accurate, understandable documentation is still as important as ever to any system development activity. Poor documentation at any stage will still cause a poor-quality product to be delivered because of the resultant poor communication between developers and users. It is likely also, if the documentation is inadequate, that the system will be difficult and expensive to maintain. (This is a good rule of thumb to apply when purchasing packaged software, also.)

But you might be saddled with maintaining or updating some existing systems that were never well documented and that contain acres of the infamous spaghetti code. If you really cannot just throw this stuff away (or get another job), there are an increasing number of reverse engineering or reengineering tools that can at least get you started on the process of providing some documentation and easier to read code from those old, cobwebbed products.

So, again, ensure that good, consistent, complete documentation of the system is produced at all system development stages. Also, have this documentation reviewed by the project development team, including the users, at regular intervals.

Realize, however, that many systems professionals really do not like writing anything except program code. Also, many of these folks have been using the advent of more automated forms of system creation as excuses for neglecting human-readable documentation. So, persuading the project team to produce more and better documentation than it is accustomed to doing may be a difficult task. But, if successful, it *will* be worth the effort.

1.2.3 Poor Communication

Successful system development will always depend on the successful interaction among various diverse groups within an enterprise. This interaction itself depends on good communication between these groups. Communication will take many forms: written, spoken, graphic symbols, program listings, and even body language. If good communication is not maintained among all the involved groups, misunderstandings will inevitably occur. These misunderstandings will lead to the wrong documents being used as specifications, design documents, and the like, or may lead to beliefs that the system has been successfully tested when in fact it has not. Often, inadequate funding for a project is a direct result of the fact that good, understandable, documentation about the project was not presented to upper management. (And, of course, lack of good documentation will cause the project to cost more, using up that inadequate funding even more quickly.) Poor communication is often responsible for more of the problems in a system development project than any other factor. When large projects require interaction among large numbers of people and organizations, good communication becomes paramount in importance, and some formalized, regular communication on the project's progress becomes essential.

Regular reviews of progress, walk-throughs of deliverables, and simple progress and status reports are all good methods of communicating the necessary data about a project. These activities must be built into the project life cycle.

1.2.4 Overambitious Objectives

Several system development projects that I have known, and even been involved with, have failed because of sheer size. (I'm sure that you can enumerate at least one such project that you have heard of.) In such cases, the simple enormity of the set of (highly laudable) objectives ensured that the system would not get delivered before the world had moved on significantly and the need for the system had simply evaporated or had been met by different, more state of the art technology. Or the task of developing such an enormous system proved to be simply too much for the existing technology or available resources. In fact, Brook's law (reference 4) asserts that, after a certain size has been reached, adding members to the project team will *increase* the time required to complete the project merely because of the additional administration and communication required.

Breaking down the project into manageable pieces and then treating each piece as a *separate* project, with an overall understanding of how they all fit together, is a conceptual way of handling this problem. A good rule of thumb is to insist that no project may last longer than 12 months.

1.2.5 Low Quality, Poor Performance

Poor performance is often caused, as are many negative system characteristics, by inadequate analysis and definition of the system's requirements.

Particularly in today's environment, there is an enormous temptation to go ahead with an expensive system installation purely on the basis of a successful prototype. Developing an effective PC- or workstation-based prototype of a real-time, on-line transaction processing system with four or five friendly selected users is very different than developing the same system to run in an environment with hundreds or thousands of terminal or workstation users accessing the same databases, and *all* requiring subsecond response time and accurate, 100% reliable availability and backup of all transactions and data. Also, many application generators still produce code that stands up perfectly well in preproduction testing but cannot handle the day in, day out rigors of daily production.

Quality is defined by Crosby (reference 2) as being "conformance to specifications." Again, if the specifications are not clear and comprehensive, the quality of the system will also never be well defined, and therefore, human nature being what it is, the quality of the system will be unacceptable.

Therefore, at the start of the system life cycle, *insist* on good, clear, understandable specifications. These specifications must include practical, achievable performance and quality criteria. Then, well *before* going into production, ensure that the system is fully tested for accuracy and reliability, and successfully against all performance criteria and all user requirements.

1.2.6 Never-ending Development

This recipe for failure is related to item 4, overambitious obectives. Often, a project is so large and complex that it simply seems to go on forever. Also, an additional factor that can produce this situation is the overeagerness of the development organization to please the user. We have all met the systems developer for whom the answer to every request for more functionality or performance is "no problem!" Unfortunately, there is a problem—the system will never be finished. Application system development projects are not to be treated as academic theses; as mentioned earlier, a project is defined as an activity with a *finite* end date.

So, if a project looks as if it may never end, start breaking it up into manageable pieces, each of which can be regarded as a separate, though connected, project. If you can, assign a separate project manager to each of these smaller subprojects. This may also have the effect of saving time, because the subprojects may be carried out in parallel to some extent. Also, get tough with the user and make it clear that extra requirements will require extra effort, expenses, and time. *There is no free lunch!* Suggest that later *versions* may be the place for the delivery of the extra requirements. This is another strong argument for heavy involvement of the user at all stages of system development, especially at the reviews of the end-stage deliverables.

1.2.7 High Costs and Cost Overruns

The initial cost of a project relates directly to the length of time taken to deliver the system and the amount of resources expended over the total system life cycle. But the costs of actually running the delivered system in production will normally be the largest part of the total life cycle costs. Obviously, as data processing professionals we must attempt at all times to develop cost-effective systems. A system delivered with the minimum amount of errors will require less maintenance in production and therefore will be more cost effective than one with a larger relative number of mistakes. In addition, and as important, is the need to estimate with some acceptable accuracy how much the system will cost to develop and operate and how long the development activity will take. Many of the endemic cost overruns result from totally unrealistic estimates at the start of projects.

Therefore, in addition to managing the system development project *like any other business activity* by controlling costs and expenses with regular reviews of progress, accurate estimates of the total and any remaining costs must be carried out continuously. This presupposes an accepted and accurate estimating method. The first step in developing a reliable estimating methodology is to have a consistent, measurable way of conducting the system development activities. *Perhaps, if we had reliable estimates, many projects would never get started.*

1.2.8 Perpetual Maintenance

IBM's Operating Systems Software packages are subject to "perpetual" maintenance. Well, *nearly* perpetual. In these particular cases, this amount of maintenance is probably necessary because of the constant stream of new features that the millions of users demand. (And that IBM insists they need!) But, in the slightly less demanding world of business applications software, there is often less excuse for some of the constant changes that occur to production systems. The high level of maintenance work that goes on is a drain on valuable resources that could be used in developing some of the new systems that are currently sitting impatiently in the "system development backlog."

What *is* this thing called maintenance? A computer program does not need a 4000 mile checkup, there are no moving parts, no spark plugs to change, no batteries to replace. So what are all these systems maintenance people doing?

A large part, and sometimes the largest part, of maintenance activity on production systems actually consists of what systems people euphemistically call "fixing bugs." Thanks to Admiral Grace Hopper, programmers' mistakes are universally called bugs. My belief is that by calling their mistakes bugs, perhaps programmers somehow subconsciously imply that the mistakes are not really their responsibility; they "crept" into the software all on their own. (I know Admiral Hopper would not fall into that trap; after all, *she* found a *real* bug, a moth.)

Much of the estimated 60% to 70% and more of systems costs that are spent on maintenance could be eliminated by not *designing* so many mistakes. Effective management and technical reviews of the interim system development deliverables, documentation and code, could eliminate many of the bugs currently delivered into production. Also, comprehensive, intelligently applied testing, *throughout* the development life cycle, is also a key factor in delivering quality, error-free code. Zero-defect production is an achievable objective in many industries today; we in the systems development industry should make it our objective also.

Finally, there is increasingly a bewildering array of automated tools to help us deliver applications code faster and with fewer errors. Many applications designers and particularly many operating systems programmers still insist that these tools cannot help in delivering high-peformance systems. However, the Luddites did not stop the Industrial Revolution, and these latter-day naysayers will not stop the current revolution in their own industry either.

Ultimately, all applications software and much systems software will be delivered either as single off-the-shelf packages, as combinations of existing software objects from an object-oriented repository, or by extensive use of nonprocedural languages and application generators. The increased use of these system development techniques will cause a corresponding decrease in bugs, increases in system development productivity and system quality, and a decrease in the amount of maintenance necessary.

1.3 HOW PROJECT MANAGEMENT CAN HELP

With all these possible causes of failure and probably many more not mentioned, what can you, the systems development project manager, do? If there are political reasons that are likely to cause project failure, as discussed in reference 3, the best available action may be to brush up your résumé. But, assuming that there is no nefarious activity going on to sabotage your project in order to further some organizational pirate's career, a number of things can be done to provide at least a reasonable chance of success. As you might have guessed, a lot of the things you can do fall under the general description of project management.

1.3.1 Divide and Conquer

Divide the project up into manageable chunks. Subscribe to the *concept* of several sequential stages of activities with clear, *measurable* end-stage deliverables preceded in each case by small *measurable, monitorable* tasks leading up to the creation of the major stage deliverable (see Figure 1.1a). Recognize that the concept of sequential stages is just that, a *concept* only. In real life there will and should be a significant amount of overlap across stages, parallel activities, and, most importantly, iteration of stages and in-stage activities (see Figure 1.1b). In today's world, there is no such thing as a "frozen" specification, design, or set of requirements. Somebody, somewhere, *all* the time will be rapidly thawing these frozen items, officially or unofficially. So, make it official! The effect of that, of course, is to make the management task more difficult, which is even more reason to have an agreed-on project management process.

Under the same concept of divide and conquer, if even when divided into stages the project is still too big to be adequately managed, by mere mortals, consider dividing it into several separate *projects*. This may result in cost-effective synergies by introducing even more opportunities for parallel activities, with attendant time savings and more efficient resource utilization (see Figure 1.1c). Of course, *someone* must be given the responsibility of coordinating the total set of activities and ensuring that the whole thing comes together at the end.

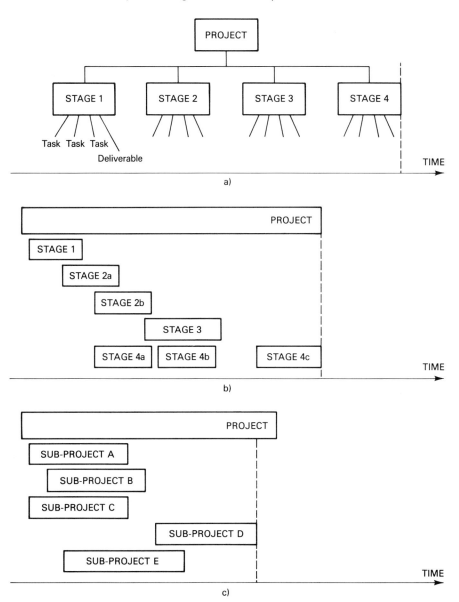

Figure 1.1   Breaking Up the Project

1.3.2 Measurable Deliverables

Define clearly the *minimum* set of *measurable* deliverables required to be completed at the end of each system development stage. These deliverables serve at least three important purposes:

1. To provide a set of components, documentation, code, and the like, that will together be the final delivered product.
2. To provide a means to measure progress and the quality (conformance to specifications) of the developing product.
3. To provide a set of starting conditions for the next stage's activities.

It is very likely that there will be many interim deliverables within each stage in addition to the major end-stage deliverables. Ensure that the production of these deliverables is also monitored and measured, as well as the major items delivered at the ends of stages. All deliverables will probably require activity that spans across several stages.

1.3.3 Reviews and Walk-throughs

Set up regular management and technical reviews of all deliverables and of progress. However, do *not* wait for a deliverable to be completed in each case before carrying out a review. The review may never happen. Software products are infamous for being "90% complete" from here to eternity.

Identify some of the regular scheduled reviews as reestimation and go/no go points. (Chapter 5 provides suggestions for these review points.) At these points in the project's schedule, the project can be canceled! Make this clear to all concerned and have these particular reviews at the end of each stage as a *minimum*.

Set up a process for handling unacceptable deliverables. Reworking, selection of alternatives, and cancellation of the project are all options at this point. Also, install a process for emergency technical and management reviews for when things start to fall apart.

Determine the role of quality assurance and audit in the project, particularly at the reviews. In my opinion, quality assurance should be involved consistently throughout the project's life cycle, starting no later than at the design reviews. Their involvement should be on a consultancy basis in the early stages, leading up to active involvement during the final testing of the system.

1.3.4 Testing

Set up a minimum acceptable set of tests for all modules and the complete system and make it clear that this set is an *unassailable* minimum. This minimum set should be defined by a consensus among the system's users, developers, quality assurance testers, and DP audit, or a similarly representative group. The results from this level of testing must be sufficient to convince this group of the system's readiness for production. (See reference 1 for a full description of the testing required.)

1.3.5 Project Staffing

Recognize that a successful system development project results from, above all else, having the right people in the required positions. A fairly wide variety of skills is essential in all such projects, and such skills will not all reside in one person or even in one department. Identify these skills in relation to the specific deliverables and also identify the potential sources of these skills.

Most importantly, as early as possible, assign a project manager who understands and is good at, surprisingly enough, project management. Don't make the mistake of assuming that the best systems analyst or system designer will be the best project manager. These people probably will not be and, more importantly, will almost certainly not *want* to be project managers. Increasingly today, the project manager is being assigned from the user organization, a highly favorable trend. On large, complex projects, if you *must* have such things, assign *two* project managers, one each from the user and development organizations, with the user project manager having seniority in the project hierarchy. In this case, the user and development project managers might be called the project executive and project manager, respectively. Insist that one of the project manager's earliest responsibilities is to determine the human, machine, and other material resources needed for the project and to decide on the organization of the project team.

A final note on the role of the project manager: In today's increasingly complex and matrixed organizations, a well-developed ability to effectively interact with and motivate widely disparate groups is probably the project manager's most important and most required characteristic.

1.3.6 Change Control

Set up a procedure for handling changes to the required system, both during development and in production. In today's dynamic business environment, any project whose development lasts longer than two weeks will have different requirements when it is delivered from when it was conceived. Business needs, technological capabilities, and organizational requirements will all change over time, forcing changes in all business and information systems.

If you are *very* lucky, there will be an existing, effective change-control procedure available for your use. In any case, try to identify a suitable software package to control access to and levels of database generations, software libraries, and the like. Such a package can be invaluable in the effective control of software changes and releases. This effective control or management of the components and release levels of a software system is often referred to as *software configuration management.*

1.3.7 Maintenance

Once the system is finally installed into the production environment, the job of managing related activities does not end. Basically, change control is mostly what maintenance is all about, and each batch of changes must be handled as a project, with *exception* procedures for handling emergency situations. But, in addition, there is the monitoring of the operation of the system to ensure that it continues to meet the user's requirements.

Ideally, set up a generic *service level agreement* (SLA), which, before the system is completed, will be customized, agreed with, and signed by the developers, users, and eventual system operators. The monitoring of and management of deviations from this agreement will be a major system maintenance activity. This activity should be managed as a project, on a regular basis, each such project being defined as "Management of the Service Level Agreement for System A for 1993," for example. The SLA project will then be reinitiated, with the details of the agreement reviewed at the start of each year or on a more frequent basis if necessary.

The service level agreement should include such items as the following:

- System performance
    Transaction response time

        Transaction turnaround time
        System throughput

- Timeliness of reports, statements, and the like
- Accuracy of information generated
- System Availability (percentage of "up time")
- Mean time between failures (MTBF)
- Mean time to repair (MTTR)
- User satisfaction
- Operational costs
- Timeliness and effectiveness of new functionality installations

Each item must have an agreed-on quantitative method of measurement and an agreed-on satisfactory level of that measurement, for example, 95% minimum system availability for an on-line system or less than 1-second transaction response time for a transaction processing system.

The service level agreement must be monitored on a regular basis. Some items, such as availability, may need to be monitored continuously. All measured items should be reported regularly, probably at no less than a monthly frequency. In addition, all items on the SLA must be reviewed regularly for continued relevance and deleted or added to, as necessary. This review should be carried out at least yearly.

The preceding is a minimum set of requirements to get started on the job of managing the system development task. This book will concentrate on the specific topic of project management. In subsequent Chapters 2 through 5, I provide more detailed help in project management by further defining the specific system development life cycle stages and their contained activities and by suggesting some practical, inexpensive management tools to make project management easier. The main intention of this book is for it to be a highly practical tool for the project manager. It should serve as a daily reference for *what* to do next and *how* to do it, even down to providing ready to use forms and checklists (see Chapters 4 and 5).

Chapter 6 discusses the estimating techniques currently in use, with their advantages and drawbacks. Chapter 7 shows how the generic life cycle defined in Chapter 2 must change to accommodate the state of the art tools now available. Finally, Chapter 8 looks at the future needs of project management in the software development arena. Will we even need to worry about managing such projects?

You will have detected from the foregoing discussion that the elements of project management discussed so far are directly related to solving the problems that cause project failure. All the wonderful technical advances that we have seen and will continue to see in the world of data processing have not yet assured a corresponding increase in on-time, underbudget, high-quality systems. I believe this is partly because the development of these systems has still not been managed adequately. In short, we need to provide the same upgrades in project management techniques as we have seen in hardware production and we are about to see in the production of software. This book provides a starting point, at least, for these upgrades.

A more detailed discussion of all of the elements of the systems development life cycle, including system and program design, testing, and coding, can be found in reference 1.

2

CONCEPTS OF THE SYSTEM DEVELOPMENT LIFE CYCLE

"Begin at the beginning" the King said gravely, "and go till you come to the end; then stop."

Lewis Carroll, *Alice's Adventures in Wonderland,* 1865

From the introduction to project management given in Chapter 1, we should be able to define what goes into a generic system development life cycle. This life cycle should then be applicable to almost any software system development project. In fact, such a life cycle should be generally applicable to *any* project involved in constructing something. Many textbooks on project management use the analogy of building a house to explain the need for a life cycle and its related project management activities. The major difference between building a house and creating a software system, is however, a significant difference. Everyone knows what a house looks like; it is tangible and familiar. This is not true for a software system; even when it is completed, it cannot really be seen. For this and other reasons covered in Chapter 1, the process of building a software system is fraught with perception-related difficulties that can largely be overcome by using a detailed set of monitoring and measuring techniques, otherwise known as a system development methodology.

2.1 Requirements for a Good System Development Methodology

Essentially, all *system development methodologies* (SDMs) are formal sets of rules for subdividing the complete system development effort into a manageable set of discrete tasks. These methodologies can take the form of manuals with forms and checklists, or they can be provided as a software package that automatically prompts the project team when tasks must be started and completed.

The methodology can be purchased or it can be developed in house. Generally, it is cheaper in the short term to purchase a prepackaged methodology because the development time for a complete, in-house version is prohibitive. Any purchased methodology will, however, normally be extensively and continuously customized for use in any one environment. Also, the complete set of documentation provided with the purchased package may represent far more in the way of procedures and standards than the organization can handle at the current time. Therefore, much work will be required to modify and customize this documentation to make it compatible with the installing organization's environment. So, by the time that the purchased SDM is fully ready for use, it may have actually cost as much as an in-house methodology, and it will probably never be *exactly* what was needed or wanted. The most cost-effective approach may be to take a published *summary* of a practical SDM, for example a list of stages, tasks, and deliverables, and use that as a starting point.

Whichever acquisition or creation approach is taken, the chosen SDM must have at least the following characteristics:

- Discrete stages (not necessarily sequential)
- Stage-limited commitment
- Sign off of interim end products
- In-stage and end-stage reviews
- Generic task lists
- Review boards or committees

Also, the SDM must enable the project manager to ask and get satisfactory answers to

- *What?* (are we creating)
- *When?* (will we deliver it)

- *Who?* (is responsible for what pieces)
- *How much?* (will it cost)

for all the stage deliverables and the final end product whenever during the system development life cycle these questions are asked.

2.1.1 Discrete Stages of the Life Cycle

The life cycle must consist of a series of stages, each of which is distinguished by the activities performed and completed within the stage and by a specific end-stage product, usually in the form of documentation. This end product serves as input for the next stage.

But, even though the stages proceed *conceptually* in a sequential fashion, it is very important to realize that there will be iteration among the stages of many of the included tasks and that there will likely be repetition of some of the actual stages themselves. Also, as mentioned in Chapter 1, some tasks will extend across stages. Figure 2.1 demonstrates the general idea of stages. Figure 2.2 illustrates the idea of *feedback,* which will entail much iteration when new and changed requirements surface as a result of both users and developers discovering more about the system as it develops. Prototyping techniques will particularly require the acceptance of iteration in the life cycle (see Chapter 7).

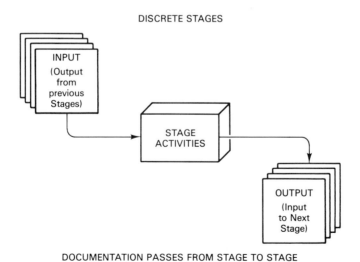

DISCRETE STAGES

DOCUMENTATION PASSES FROM STAGE TO STAGE

Figure 2.1   Discrete Stages

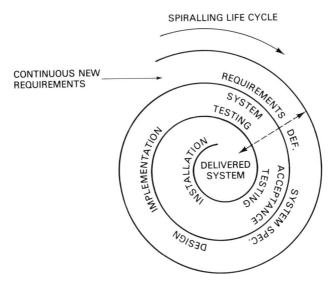

Figure 2.2 Spiralling Life Cycle

Also, it is important to realize that the life cycle of any software application system is probably closer to a spiral than a set of sequential events (Figure 2.2). Starting at the outside with the early requirements and design activities and then circling repetitively around through design, implementation, and testing, the cycle finally spirals into a delivered product. Throughout the spiral, there is interaction between adjacent layers. For example, while early versions are being installed, either as prototypes or early production models, more design work is being carried out to improve these installed versions. In addition, new requirements are continuously entered at the start of the spiral.

2.1.2 Stage-limited Commitment

Stage-limited commitment implies a commitment, in terms of detailed costs and schedules, for the next sequential stage only. This limited commitment recognizes that estimating the complete costs and schedules for the total project is very difficult and subject to constant change as the project unfolds and the developers and users find out more about the needs of the evolving system. The estimates are reviewed at the end of each stage and, if necessary, the Cost/Benefit Analysis is redone. This type of limited commitment is sometimes referred to as a *creeping commitment*. (See Chapter 4 for estimating techniques.)

2.1.3 Sign off of Stage End Products

At the end of each stage, the stage end product is reviewed by all involved organizations. One major comparison to be made is between the product and the end-product of the previous stage. The planned trend throughout the life cycle is for the end products to become progressively more detailed, more explicit, more accurate, and more refined until the final end product is the system itself. So the comparison between any stage's input and its output is part of the essential feedback mechanism that ensures close adherence to the users' needs (see Figure 2.3). In addition, the end-stage review monitors how the developing product continues to match the changing needs of the ever-changing DP and business environment. (See the section "Review Boards or Committees" later in this chapter for the recommended members of the review committee.)

If the end product is found to be satisfactory, it will be signed off by the Review Committee and the commencement of the next stage will be of-

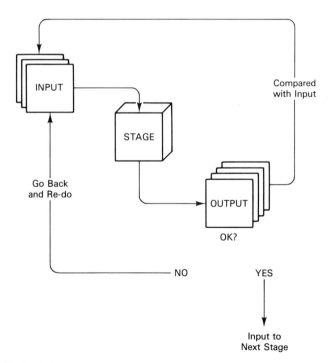

Figure 2.3   Feedback Concept

ficially approved. In actual practice, the next stage will have probably already started in order to not lose any time. It can always be stopped if a problem is found with the previous stage's end product.

2.1.4 In-stage Reviews

In addition to the end-stage reviews described previously, there will be a number of points within each stage when sufficient interim end products have been produced to have a "minireview." Progress, as well as products, can be the subject of these in-stage reviews, which will necessarily be less formal than the end-stage events. The walk-through technique, described in reference 1, is useful in some of these situations.

2.1.5 Generic Task Lists

Clearly, the set of tasks that must be carried out in order to develop a system is very similar whatever system is being developed. The good SDM will provide a set of generic tasks that will fit any system development situation. Normally, any one system development project will not require all the listed tasks. In this way, a consistent development approach is maintained, and the danger of forgetting any required tasks is minimized. *The task list is the heart of the SDM!* (see Figure 2.4).

2.1.6 Review Boards or Committees

Certain business functions are *always* affected by the development and implementation of major data processing applications. The DP development and support organization and the end users of the applications are obviously affected (see Figure 2.5). Also, the DP operations organization will be affected by the implementation of a new system. Less obvious, perhaps, is the financial control organization, often referred to as the *controllers*. This function usually has the responsibility of ensuring that the enterprise's funds are being distributed and consumed wisely. Some systems will have direct impact on other entities, such as customers, other business functions, and marketing organizations.

All the preceding organizations, when affected by the system being developed, should be represented on a review board or committee that itself has the responsibility of reviewing the system products at the end-stage reviews. Quality assurance, if it exists, should also be represented *as a function separate from system development.*

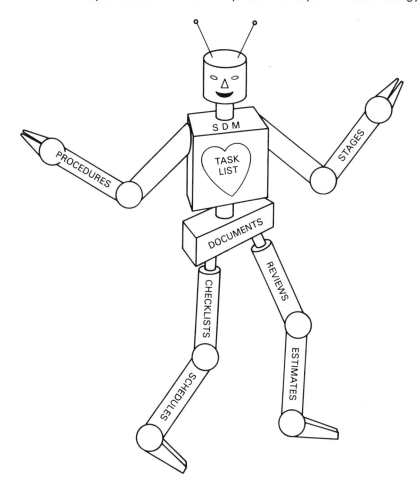

Figure 2.4   The Task List Is the "Heart" of the Systems Development Methodology

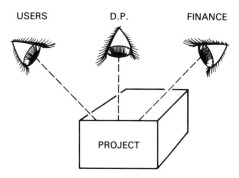

Figure 2.5   Review Board or Committees

Each end-stage review should examine, in detail, the contents of the major stage end product(s). The end-stage deliverables list in Chapter 4 could be used as a basis for the reviews. These deliverables should be reviewed for completeness, accuracy, acceptability by all reviewers, and conformance with the overall requirements of the system being developed.

Important Note: The full system development methodology should be regarded as an encyclopedia. We do not need to read it each time that a project task is carried out; but it is available as a reference, and the project manager should know the structure of the SDM and where to look for guidance when he needs it.

2.2 RULES OF THUMB

The following rules of thumb are some practical steps that can be taken by project management to ensure effective use of the SDM.

1. Review carefully the recommended list of tasks at the start of each stage to ensure their relevancy to the task at hand. Remove any that are not relevant to your project. (*But,* review *any* planned removals of tasks, as appropriate, with systems development, the user, quality assurance, and your peers.)
2. Limit the length of the project to 12 months as an absolute maximum. If the project will be much longer than that, then you have *more than one* manageable project.
3. Ensure that each major stage produces at least one major deliverable, usually in the form of documentation, and that a stage manager is appointed to be responsible for the creation of that end product and for management of all related activities and tasks.
4. Review each stage's major deliverable before making any irreversible decisions for or in the next stage.
5. If a task can be safely carried out earlier than the SDM implies, then do it, assuming the necessary resources are available. Remember that the documentary placing of a task or activity within a stage means only that this task or activity should be *completed* in that stage. It could be *started* at any convenient earlier time.
6. Review the Cost/Benefit Analysis at the end of each stage and repeat it

if the project estimates or assumptions have changed. (This often means that this analysis needs to be repeated at the end of each stage to ensure that the financial justification for the project is still valid.)

7. Remember that the life cycle stages and tasks are *guidelines* only. Do not let the SDM run the project. It is *normal* to revisit some of the stages several times. It is also *normal* to eliminate some of the tasks as being irrelevant to the project.

8. Hold weekly status meetings with the project team. This helps to focus on objectives and to maintain a positive team atmosphere. *Something* should be worth reporting each week or *something* is wrong.

3

LIFE CYCLE STAGES

Any new venture goes through the following stages: Enthusiasm, Complication, Disillusionment, Search for the Guilty, Punishment of the Innocent, and Promotion of the non-involved.

Anonymous

My version of the generic system development life cycle has eight stages:

1. Feasibility study
2. Requirements definition
3. System specification
4. System design
5. Program design and development
6. System test
7. Implementation and production
8. Maintenance

These stages may change in number and name in various proprietary system development methodologies and in different organizations, but the overall set of tasks and activities included in these stages should remain basically the same whatever methodology is used. Stated differently, this life cycle contains a series of activities (the generic task list) that must be carried out, or at least considered, each time a system is developed. Let's look at these activities in more detail, stage by stage.

3.1 FEASIBILITY STUDY

The objective of the feasibility study is to prove the practicability of the proposed system. This stage is usually carried out before full funding is approved. Normally, it is the shortest and least costly of all the stages. It can become longer and more expensive if the proposed system is not well supported with financial and need-based justification.

A useful starting point for the feasibility study is often a completed *Project Request Form,* as shown in the accompanying example.

The feasibility study should produce the following as its output:

- A *brief* description of the proposed system and its characteristics.
- A *brief* description of the business need for the proposed system.
- A proposed organizational structure defining the responsibilities of the project team.
- A cost/benefit analysis, including a gross estimate of schedules and costs and a payback schedule.
- A proposed, tentative schedule for the delivery of key stage deliverables.

Therefore, the activities to be carried out during the feasibility study are as follows:

- Analyze the proposed system and produce a written description.
- Develop a statement of the probable types of system: centralized, decentralized, mainframe based, PC based, and so on.
- Analyze the costs of similar systems, internal and external to the specific business or organization.
- Produce a rough estimate of the system size, costs, schedules, and the like.
- Define the benefits of the proposed system and develop the initial payback schedule.

MEGABUCK INC - DATA PROCESSING GROUP
PROJECT REQUEST FORM

Project Name: On-line Sales Report......   <u>Date:</u> 01/02/91..........

<u>Statement of Need:</u> – Example -

Develop an on-line system for Megabuck's regional sales managers to monitor daily,
monthly, and year-to-date sales of multiple Megabuck products.

<u>Required Implementation Date:</u>   12/31/92

<u>Compatibility Required with any Existing System(s) ?</u>.

   (Circle relevant reply)   YES/NO

<u>If YES, list system(s)</u>

Batch Sales Reporting System
....
....
....

<u>Responsible business manager(s)</u>

   (Signature, date, organizational stamp)
....
....
....

<u>DP group project manager(s) assigned</u>

   <u>Signature:</u> ....   <u>Date:</u>...........................
               ....
               ....

<u>Business project manager assigned</u>

   <u>Signature:</u> ....   <u>Date:</u>...........................
               ....
               ....

<u>PROJECTED COMPLETION DATE FOR FEASIBILITY STUDY</u>

   <u>Date:</u> ....   <u>Signed:</u>........................ DP
                                                 .... Business

----

- Produce a detailed estimate of the next life cycle stage (requirements definition).
- Assign the project manager(s).
- Present the feasibility study document to management (or review committee) for approval.

3.2 REQUIREMENTS DEFINITION

In this stage, the brief description of the proposed system from the feasibility study is expanded into a comprehensive set of user requirements. Usually, through a series of interviews with the current users (if there is a current system) and proposed users of the new system, a detailed analysis of the current and proposed system requirements is produced. This set of requirements must be written in clear, non-DP language so that future readers can easily see what the proposed system is supposed to do and how it will differ from any existing system.

In addition, a prototype may be produced at this stage as a means of obtaining accurate feedback from the potential end users as to how the system should look and feel. This prototype will consist of a believable simulation of the screens, inputs, and outputs of the system, along with the expected performance. It should be constructed for easy changes so that it can be modified quickly upon users' requests.

The output from this stage contains the following:

- An analysis of the current system (if any). (*Important:* This analysis need only be to the depth required to determine the scope and functions of the new system.)
- A detailed set of new system user requirements.
- A summary description of the proposed system.
- Estimates of the next stage and of the remainder of the project.
- An index to all related material.

A summary of the activities needed to derive the preceding outputs is given in Figure 3.1. The details of these activities are described in the task lists for the requirements definition stage in Chapter 4.

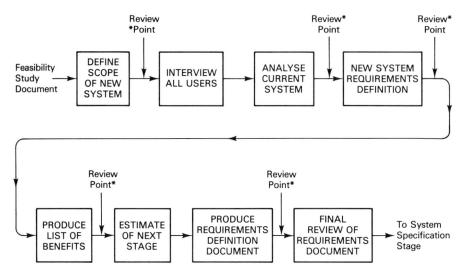

Figure 3.1   Requirements Definition Stage Activities

3.3 SYSTEM SPECIFICATION

The system specification stage contains the activities required to translate the user requirements produced in the previous stage into more DP-oriented language. In particular, the information requirements are translated into *data* requirements. This activity will build the first entries into the system data dictionary and will start the database design tasks, at least at an outline level.

The output from this stage is the system specification document, which contains the following:

- System description
- Data requirements
- Network and telecommunications requirememts
- System controls (password access, recovery/restart, and so on)
- Revised cost/benefit analysis and payback schedule
- Estimates of the next stage and of the remainder of the project
- An index to all related material

The System Specification itself may well be expressed in terms of data flow diagrams (DFDs), and the system test plan should be started at this stage by the users in the project team.

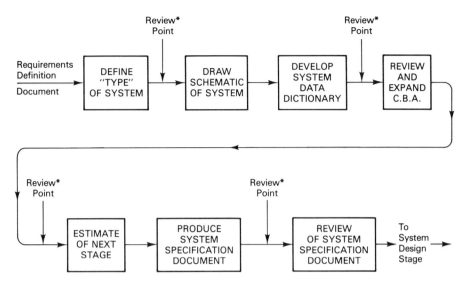

Figure 3.2   System Specification Stage Activities

Figure 3.2. provides a summary of the activities required in the system specification stage. The details of these activities are described in the task lists for the system specification stage in Chapter 4.

3.4 SYSTEM DESIGN

This important stage produces a complete technical description of the proposed system. This description must be detailed enough for the programmers in the next stage to create their programs from it directly.

Decisions must be made by the end of this stage as to which, if any, of the parts of the proposed system must be developed in house, which can be implemented by purchased, off-the-shelf software, and which can be developed by external organizations. If reusable code modules or object-oriented development techniques are being used, this is the stage where the specific modules and/or objects to be integrated must be identified.

The data administrator and the database administrator must be involved at this stage, and the final system design must include a complete logical *and* physical database design and a list of all required entries in the system data dictionary, with cross references to the corporate data dictionary, if any.

The outputs from this stage must include the following:

- A management summary of the proposed system.
- A detailed system description, including descriptions and specifications of:
  Programs, modules, objects, and the like
  Files and databases
  Records and transactions
  Data dictionary
  Procedures
  Schedules and timings
  Interfaces, both human and machine
- A description of the proposed system controls.
- A revised cost–benefit analysis and payback schedule.
- Recommended design alternatives: prototyping techniques, phased development, and so on.
- Recommended program design techniques and programming and documentation standards.
- Recommended implementation techniques, self-code, purchased or precoded packages or external development, and so on.
- A preliminary system test plan.
- Estimates of the next stage and of the remainder of the project.
- An index to related material.

A summary of the activities needed to derive all the outputs listed for system design and to ensure the technical and business integrity of the design are illustrated in Figure 3.3. The details of these activities are described in the task lists for the system design stage in Chapter 4.

3.5 PROGRAM DESIGN AND DEVELOPMENT

This stage is normally where all the *programming* is done. The program specifications produced in the previous, system design stage are used as a basis to create the programs that make up the proposed system. Usually, a great deal of additional design at the program level is also carried out here.

All programs written are fully tested before being integrated into the growing framework of the system. Completed programs are tested in conjunction with other related programs in a process known as *integration*

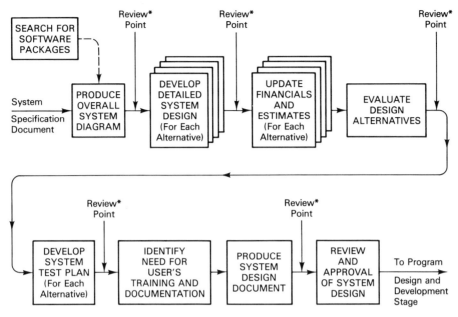

Figure 3.3   System Design Stage Activities

testing. The final integration test will consist of all the system's programs finally running together.

The amount of work needed in this stage depends a great deal on the type of programming languages being used. The use of a high-level programming language, reusable code, or object-oriented techniques will cause this stage to proceed much faster than if a low-level language is used. Additionally, if prototyping techniques and/or application generators are used, this stage will be potentially greatly shortened and perhaps completely eliminated (see Chapter 7).

In addition to the programs, databases, and files, the user procedures and documentation must be produced and tested in this stage so that the users are confident that they can run the new system without constant help from the DP department. The program and system documentation must also be completed to standards so that future changes and maintenance can be carried out with ease.

The end products from this stage must include the following:

- Detailed design documents for the system and for *each* program.
- Detailed design diagrams for the system and for *each* program.

- Detailed logic descriptions for each program.
- Detailed program documentation for each program.
- Input–output descriptions (files, databases, transactions, screens, reports, and the like).
- Program source listings, including embedded comments.
- Job control language (JCL or equivalent) listings, if necessary.
- Operator's guide for the *complete* system.
- Results of unit tests for each program.
- Results of integration tests.
- User training program and manuals.
- Operator training program and manuals.
- User guide for the *complete* system.
- Estimates of next stages, including the implementation schedule, the conversion plan, and the recovery/contingency plan.
- System test plan.
- Index to related material.

Figure 3.4 summarizes the activities needed to produce the outputs for this stage and to ensure the technical and business accuracy and integrity of the system and programs produced. A detailed set of activities is given in the task lists for the program design and development stage in Chapter 4.

3.6 SYSTEM TEST

If all the testing designated to be carried out in previous stages has been done correctly and comprehensively, the system test should be a formality. Sadly, this is not often the case. However, this is usually the first time that the user has seen the complete system working, so it is important that the system test be as comprehensive as possible, irrespective of how much repetition of previous tests this entails.

Three major objectives are intended to be met by the system test stage:

1. Satisfying the full users' requirements. A full and comprehensive test, carried out by the DP staff and supervised by the users, is the normal way to meet this objective.

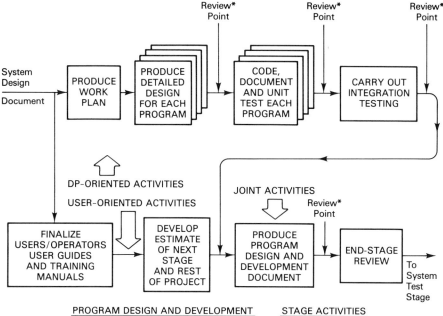

Figure 3.4   Program Design and Development Stage Activities

2. Ensuring that the new system meets the users' acceptance criteria. This objective is often met by the system being run through its paces by a team of DP operators, controlled by the users.

3. Ensuring that the system will operate satisfactorily in the production environment. Often, the first two objectives will have been met by running the new system in a test, nonproduction environment. This final objective must be met by using the production level files, databases, programs, procedures, and manuals. Also, the production staff expected to operate the system must conduct this part of the test.

These major objectives of system testing are most often met by carrying out three separately managed test activities, one after the other, using different test teams as indicated. In carrying out these tests, the following specific testing needs must be met.

- Testing the systems's full requirements against the system requirements definition

- Volume testing
- Stress testing
- Configuration testing
- Documentation testing

The outputs from the system test stage must include the following:

- System Test Plan (Updated).
- System test results.
- Results at variance with the expected results and plans for resolution of these variances.
- Results of documentation tests.
- Implementation schedule, conversion plan and recovery, contingency, and fallback plans.
- Letter of system approval, signed by the end-user organization.
- Service level agreement (defining expected levels of system service agreed on by the system operations, support, and the user).
- Index to related material.

Figure 3.5 summarizes the activities required during the system test stage to complete the stage and to ensure that the system meets the full set of

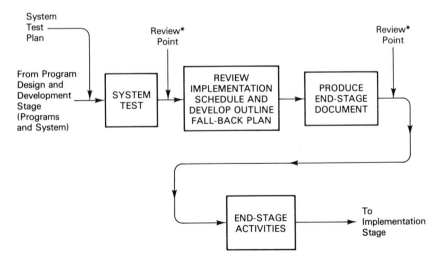

Figure 3.5 System Test Stage Activities

technical and business requirements. Full details of these activities are described in the task lists for the system test stage in Chapter 4.

3.7 IMPLEMENTATION AND PRODUCTION

When all the tests in the previous stage have been completed to the satisfaction of the users, the system is ready to be implemented. There are at least three methods of implementation:

1. *Parallel running* involves installing the new system in parallel with the existing system. The two systems are then run in parallel until the differences between the two sets of outputs are within acceptable limits. Then the old system can be "unplugged" and the new system takes over. Clearly, this style of implementation cannot be used for some online systems, and it presupposes the existence of a current system.

2. *Immediate cutover* is normally used when parallel running is impossible or unnecessary. This technique is not for the faint hearted! A quiet time in terms of production activity is usually chosen for such an implementation, and it is normally preceded by meticulous planning and even more thorough system testing than usual.

3. The *phased approach* is used when the system is large and when not all the functions of the system are needed or ready at one time. In these cases the system can be installed in separate phases over a period of time, each phase being either an immediate cutover or a parallel-run type of installation.

During the early days of production, the users have the responsibility to constantly monitor the system to ensure that it is meeting or exceeding its design criteria based on their original requirements.

After a period of time determined by the users, a postinstallation review is carried out. This usually occurs after the system becomes stable in terms of its performance and operational characteristics. This review must address at least the following items:

- Performance of the new system.
- Acceptability of the user and operator guides.
- Quality of the user and operator training manuals and training programs.

- Data conversion problems.
- Installation problems.
- Total cost of the system so far.
- Adherence to the planned schedules.

Prior to the first postimplementation review, the following deliverables must be generated and approved:

- Full set of release and maintenance procedures
- Schedule and plan for the postimplementation review
- Service level agreement among the system operation, system support, and user organizations

After completion of the postimplementation review, the following additional deliverables must be generated and approved:

- Postimplementation review report
- Schedule for further postimplementation reviews

Figure 3.6 summarizes the activities required in the implementation and production stage to ensure the user's full satisfaction with the installed

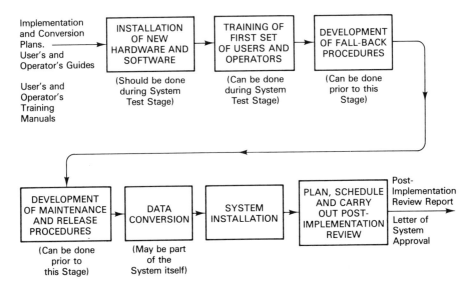

Figure 3.6 Implementation and Production Stage Activities

system. Full details of these activities can be found in the task lists for the implementation and production stage in Chapter 4.

3.8 MAINTENANCE

Once the newly installed system has survived its postimplementation review, it moves into respected adulthood and into the period of its life often euphemistically referred to as the maintenance stage. In Chapter 1 I identified two major areas of this life cycle stage:

1. Implementing changes to the system.
2. Ensuring that the system continues to meet the user's needs.

All required changes to the installed system must, in theory, be subjected to the full procedures of the system development life cycle. That is, any changes must go through the following stages:

- Feasibility study
- Requirements definition
- System specification
- System design
- Program design and development
- System test
- Implementation and production

Of course, this will not be necessary or acceptable in most cases, but the objective of ensuring that implementation of changes must be controlled is always valid. Therefore, a change-control mechanism must be implemented that ensures that the responsible management insist that each change be installed in a manner that minimizes disruption and is essentially invisible to the user of the system.

One effective way of doing this is to bundle changes into discrete releases such that each release becomes a miniproject, which is then subjected to at least a subset of the life cycle project management procedures. Systems and user management must then decide together how much of the life cycle procedurality must be applied to maintenance releases in general and each such release in particular, as necessary.

Ensuring that the system continues to meet the user requirements is best managed by use of a *service level agreement* (SLA). This document should be created by the end of the system development activities, usually before the end of the system test. It should include an agreement among all involved organizations on what performance, scheduling, recovery and restart, mean time to failure, and other operational criteria are acceptable in quantifiable terms. This document should then be monitored at an agreed-on frequency and the various monitored numbers regularly reported to relevant management. If there is a quality assurance organization, monitoring of the SLA is an effective use of that organization's resources.

Specific additional life cycle deliverables that must be generated during the maintenance stage are as follows:

- Detailed log of changes to the system
- Copies of regular reviews of the service level agreement
- Copies of regular postimplementation review reports

This chapter has described the *generic* system development life cycle. Obviously, this will be customized for each organization and, to a lesser extent, for each system development project. Nevertheless, there still remains much commonality across different organizations and projects. The next two chapters provide suggestions for practical tools to help the project manager through the life cycle.

4

TASKS AND DELIVERABLES
OF THE SYSTEM
DEVELOPMENT LIFE CYCLE

Work expands to fill the time available for its completion.

Northcote Parkinson, *Parkinson's Law,* 1962,
Houghton and Mifflin, New York, NY

This chapter provides a detailed list of the tasks to be carried out during the generic systems development life cycle and the deliverables created as a result of those tasks. These are listed in the form of documentary tools to assist in managing the generic system development life cycle described in Chapter 3. Even if you modify the generic life cycle presented here to fit your specific needs, the documents can also be modified to fit.

These checklists and recommendations are intended to be management assists. Always remember that there is no substitute for good management. The checklists and other documents will help the good project manager to be even better; the bad project manager will probably not even be reading this book!

The contents of this chapter are divided into two parts. The first section consists of the task lists for each life cycle stage. The second section describes in detail the deliverables required from each life cycle stage.

Each task list may, in fact, be used as a checklist, and they are presented that way in the rest of this chapter so that they can be directly used by the project manager and project team members.

4.1 TASK LISTS FOR EACH LIFE CYCLE STAGE

Eight task lists, one for each life cycle stage, are presented in the accompanying tables.

Task List for the Feasibility Stage

Task	Responsibility	Dates	
		Start	Finish
1. Analyze proposed system and write description			
2. Define and document possible types of system			
3. Produce cost analysis of similar systems			
4. Produce estimate of system size, schedules and costs. Include a schedule for completion of all major deliverables (See next section for deliverables)			
5. Define quantitative and qualitative benefits of the proposed system			
6. Produce initial payback schedule			
7. Produce a detailed estimate of costs, schedules, resources, and the like, for the next stage (requirements definition), including a schedule for production of the major stage deliverables			
8. Assign the project manager(s)			
9. Produce the feasibility study document (see contents list in next section)			
10. Present the feasibility study document to the management review committee for approval			

Task List for the Requirements Definition Stage

Task	Responsi-bility	Start	Finish
		Dates	

1. Define scope of proposed system:
   Functions   Dimensions
   Users   Constraints

2. Interview all current and proposed users:
   Determine: Use of current system
                Deficiencies of current system
                Requirements of new system
   Document: Current system description
                Current system deficiencies

3. Produce new system requirements document:
   Include: Prioritized user requirements (pro-
                cess and information require-
                ments)
                Resolution of current system's de-
                ficiencies

4. Produce list of tangible and intangible benefits
   (a refinement of the benefits listed in the feasibility study)

5. Produce a detailed estimate of costs, schedules,
   resources, and the like, for the next stage (system specification), including a schedule for production of the major stage deliverables

6. Produce a revised estimate of costs, schedules,
   resources, and the like, for the remainder of the
   project life cycle, including a schedule for production of the major stage deliverables

7. Produce the requirements definition document;
   this task may include the building of a prototype
   (see next section for contents of deliverables)

8. Carry out final review of requirements definition document

9. Make a decision on continuation or not of the
   project

10. Define next stage major responsibilities for
    stage manager, team members, and others

Task List for the System Specification Stage

	Responsi-	Dates	
Task	bility	Start	Finish
1. Define type of proposed system: Translate physical, environmental, and operational constraints into system characteristics (as far as is possible at this stage); for example, on-line, transaction-based? distributed or centralized? workstations or terminals?			
2. Draw a schematic of the proposed system: translate user requirements from the previous stage into functional specifications; represent these functions on the schematic			
3. Develop system data dictionary: describe all elements on system schematic, including functions *and* data (information); ensure all interfunction and interdata relationships are documented; ensure compatibility with corporate data dictionary, if it exists			
4. Review and expand cost–benefit analysis: update old cost–benefit analysis with new information; review new analysis to ensure that expected benefits still exist and that the payback period is still acceptable			
5. Produce a detailed estimate of costs, schedules, resources, and the like, for the next stage (system design), including a schedule for production of the major stage deliverables			
6. Produce a revised estimate of costs, schedules, resources, and the like, for the remainder of the project life cycle, including a schedule for production of the major stage deliverables			
7. Produce the system specification document (see next section for contents of deliverables)			
8. Carry out final review of system specification document			
9. Make decision on continuation or not of the project			
10. Define next stage major responsibilities for stage manager, team members, and others			

Task List for the System Design Stage

Task	Responsi-bility	Dates	
		Start	Finish

1. Produce overall system diagram:
   Define programs and major program functions
   Define major data flows between programs and functions
   Design data schemas, logical and physical
   Define boundaries of software packages, if any
   Define hardware and software environment, including alternatives
   Document alternative design diagrams, if appropriate

2. Search for software packages: carry out a search for suitable software packages which could implement some or all of the required system functionality in a cost-effective manner and that would, if implemented, provide an environment compatible with corporate objectives

NOTE: Activities 1 and 2 can be carried out in parallel, and activity 2 could be completed before the start of this stage.

3. Develop a detailed system design; for each design alternative:
   Provide a detailed system design narrative for the complete system and for each component, program, function, and data component
   Update the system data dictionary
   Update the corporate data dictionary (if there is one)
   Define any telecommunications equipment required and its function
   Compare the design against the system specification
   Document the required hardware and software environment

4. Update the cost–benefit analysis; for each design alternative:
   Update the cost–benefit analysis with any new information
   Review the analysis to ensure that expected benefits still exist and that the payback period is still acceptable

(continued)

Task List for the System Design Stage (continued)

Task	Responsibility	Start	Finish
		Dates	

Task	Responsibility	Start	Finish
5. Produce a detailed estimate of costs, schedules, resources, and the like, for the next stage (program design and development), including a schedule for production of the major stage deliverables			
6. Produce a revised estimate of costs, schedules, resources, and the like, for the remainder of the project life cycle, including a schedule for production of the major stage deliverables			

7. Evaluate the design alternatives; for each design alternative; document:
    User requirements being met by this alternative
    Cost–benefit analysis and payback schedule
    Probable user acceptance level
Recommend the best alternative(s)			

8. Develop system test plan:
    Create input test data
    Produce list of expected outputs
    Produce list of test criteria
    Develop system test schedule
Develop specific differential system test plans for each design alternative			

9. Identify need for user's training and documentation; define outlines for:
    Full user documentation
    Operator's manuals
    Users' and operators' training documents and schedules			

10. Produce the system design document (see next section for contents of deliverables)			
11. Carry out final review of system design document			
12. Make decision on continuation or not of the project			
13. Recommend single design alternative			
14. Make recommendation on level of involvement, if any, of subcontract programmers and others			
15. Define next stage major responsibilities for stage manager, programming and test team members, and others			

Task List for the Program Design and Development Stage

Task	Responsi-bility	Dates	
		Start	Finish

1. Produce work plan:
   > Develop detailed list of tasks to complete development and testing of all system components
   >
   > Produce schedule for all above tasks, including early and late dates and individual responsibilities (a PC-based project management system is useful for this)
   >
   > Install progress and status recording procedures
   >
   > Install time recording procedures, if appropriate
   >
   > Obtain approval of work plan from project management

2. Produce detailed design for each program:
   > Design diagrams
   > - Control flows and structures
   > - File structures
   > - Records, screens, reports, and layouts
   > - Database subschemas
   > - Table designs and layouts
   >
   > Structured English narrative
   > Narrative description of program logic
   > (The above may vary in detailed format depending on program design methods used.)

3. Code, document, and unit test each program:
   > Code programs, including all control procedures
   >
   > Carry out unit testing, iteratively if necessary, until all programs meet specifications as detailed in previous stage
   >
   > Carry out any and all necessary updates to the system and corporate data dictionaries

4. Carry out integration testing:
   > Enter successfully unit tested programs into Integration Test Library
   > Carry out integration testing on each program
   > Document all integration test results

NOTE: **Activities 1 through 4 are DP-oriented activities and should be carried out by the systems staff.**

(*continued*)

Task List for the Program Design and Development Stage
(continued)

Task	Responsi-bility	Dates Start	Finish
5. Finalize users and operators user guides and training manuals			
6. Produce a detailed estimate of costs, schedules, resources, and the like, for the next stage (system test), including a schedule for production of the major stage deliverables			
7. Produce a revised estimate of costs, schedules, resources, and the like, for the remainder of the project life cycle, including a schedule for production of the major stage deliverables			
NOTE: **Tasks 5, 6, and 7 are user-oriented tasks and should be carried out by the end-user staff and can be done in parallel with tasks 1 through 4.**			
8. Produce program design and development document (see next section for contents of deliverables)			
9. Carry out review of program design and development document			
10. Carry out review of system test plan			
11. Obtain required sign offs for completed and integration-tested programs			
12. Define next stage major responsibilities for stage manager, system test members, and others			
NOTE: **Tasks 8 through 12 are joint DP/user tasks**			

Task List for the System Test Stage

Task	Responsi-bility	Dates	
		Start	Finish
1. Carry out system test: Test system according to system test plan Check out operational use of users' and operators' guides by using them to carry out the system test Check out users' and operators' training documents by using them to train the operators and users who carry out the system test Document fully all system test results			
2. Review implementation schedule: Availability of resources Review of contingency factors that might affect implementation • End month or year special processing • Vacations and holidays Availability of third-party vendor support Final review of detailed implementation schedule			
3. Develop outline fallback plan: Criteria for fallback Identification of contingency resources Timetable for recovery or abandonment			
4. Develop service level agreement: User performance, accuracy, and volume criteria Vendor support criteria • Mean time to failure • Mean time to repair System quality criteria Frequency of measurement			
5. Produce the system test end-stage documents (see next section for contents of deliverables)			
6. Review and approve end-stage documents			
7. Approve system documentation: Program documentation Operators' manuals Users' manuals Training manuals Support documentation			

(*continued*)

Task List for the System Test Stage (continued)

Task	Responsi-bility	Start	Finish
		Dates	

8. Approve implementation plan

9. Approve contingency, recovery, and fallback plans

10. Sign off fully tested system:
    System development sign off
    Users sign off
    Operations sign off
    Quality assurance sign off
    Finance sign off

NOTE: **Tasks 6 through 10 as described above may contain some overlapping activities because approving all the system test end-stage documents (task 6) may include some of the approvals defined later in tasks 7 through 10.**

Task List for the Implementation Stage

Task	Responsi-bility	Dates	
		Start	Finish
1. Install new hardware and software (this can and should be done prior to this stage, preferably during system test)			
2. Train first set of users and operators (this should be done during the system test stage)			
3. Develop contingency, recovery, and fallback plans (this should be done during the system test stage)			
4. Develop maintenance and release procedures (this can be done prior to this stage and can be implemented via a vendor-supplied software package or with preexisting procedures used for previous systems development); set up procedures for: Regular releases* Emergency "fixes" Vendor releases (hardware and workstation) *Regular Releases of internal and vendor-supplied software should be handled like mini-projects, controlled by an agreed-on subset of the full software development life cycle.			
5. Carry out any data conversion required (this may be part of the operation of the new system)			
6. Carry out installation of new system into production: Immediate cut-over or Parallel run or Phased installation			
7. Start using service level agreement			
8. Plan and schedule the postimplementation review: Set criteria for: • System performance • System quality • User satisfaction • Quality and usability of: Users and operators manuals			

(*continued*)

Task List for the Implementation Stage (continued)

Task	Responsi-bility	Dates	
		Start	Finish
Users and operators training			
Data and information produced			
• Smoothness of installation			
• Costs of development, installation, operations, and maintenance			
Set schedule and timetable for review:			
• Ensure availability of:			
Required personnel			
Required documentation			
9. Carry out postimplementation review:			
Create postimplementation review report			
Obtain signed approval of report from:			
• System's end users			
• System operations			
• Quality assurance and audit			
• Systems development			
• System support and maintenance			
• Finance, if necessary			
Obtain letter of system approval			
10. Set schedule for further postimplementation reviews, if necessary (it is probably advisable to carry out reviews of the system, similar in content to the first postimplementation review, at regular intervals to ensure continued effectiveness of the system)			

Task List for the Maintenance Stage

Task	Responsi-bility	Dates	
		Start	Finish

1. Implement changes to the system:
    Use the release implementation procedure
    or
    Implement emergency fixes and then use formal release procedure retroactively			

2. Ensure that system continues to meet the users' needs:
    Use the service level agreement
    • Regular reviews of requirements of service level agreement
    • Regular reviews of how system is meeting those requirements
    Carry out regular reviews of the system
    • Use the procedures and contents of the postimplementation review			

4.2 DELIVERABLES REQUIRED FROM EACH LIFE CYCLE STAGE

4.2.1 Deliverables to Be Produced from the Feasibility Stage

The feasibility study should produce the following as its output:

- *Brief* description of the proposed system and its characteristics.
- *Brief* description of the business need for the proposed system.
- Proposed organizational structure defining key responsibilities of the project team.
- Cost–benefit analysis, including a gross estimate of schedules and costs and a payback schedule.
- Proposed, tentative schedule for the delivery of key stage end products.

4.2.2 Deliverables to Be Produced from the Requirements Definition Stage

The output from this stage should contain the following:

- Analysis of the current system (if any) (*Important:* This analysis need only be to the depth required to determine the scope and functions of the new system and is, of course, only required if there is an old or existing system to replace).
- Set of new system user requirements.
- Summary description of the proposed system (this can include a prototype of the proposed system).
- Estimates of the next stage and of the remainder of the project.
- Index to all related material.

4.2.3 Deliverables to Be Produced from the System Specification Stage

The output from this stage is the system specification document, which contains the following:

- System description.
- Data requirements.
- Network and telecommunications requirememts.
- System controls (password access, recovery and restart, and so on).
- Revised cost–benefit analysis and payback schedule.
- Estimates of the next stage and of the remainder of the project.
- Index to all related material.

The system specification itself may well be expressed in terms of data flow diagrams (DFDs), and the system test plan should be started at this stage by the users in the project team.

4.2.4 Deliverables to Be Produced from the System Design Stage

The outputs from this stage must include the following:

- Management summary of the proposed system.

- Detailed system description, including descriptions and specifications of the following
  Programs, reusable modules, and objects
  Files and databases
  Records and transactions
  Data dictionary
  Procedures
  Schedules and timings
  Interfaces, both human and machine
- Description of the proposed system controls.
- Revised cost–benefit analysis and payback schedule.
- Recommended design alternatives: prototyping techniques, phased development, and so on.
- Recommended program design techniques and programming and documentation standards.
- Recommended implementation techniques, self-code, purchased packages or external development, and the like.
- Preliminary system test plan.
- Estimates of the next stage and of the remainder of the project.
- Index to related material.

4.2.5 Deliverables to Be Produced from the Program Design and Development Stage

The end products from this stage must include the following:

- Detailed design documents for the system and for *each* program.
- Detailed design diagrams for the system and for *each* program.
- Detailed logic descriptions for each program.
- Detailed program documentation for each program.
- Input/output descriptions (files, databases, transactions, screens, reports, and the like).
- Program source listings, including embedded comments.
- Job control language (JCL or equivalent) listings, if necessary.
- Operator's guide for the *complete* system.
- Results of unit tests for each program.

- Results of integration tests.
- User training program and manuals.
- Operator training program and manuals.
- User guide for the *complete* system.
- Estimates of next stages, including the implementation schedule, conversion plan, and recovery and contingency plan.
- System test plan.
- Index to related material.

4.2.6 Deliverables to Be Produced from the System Test Stage

The outputs from the system test stage must include the following:

- System test plan (updated).
- System test results.
- Results at variance with the expected results and plans for resolution of these variances.
- Results of documentation tests.
- Implementation schedule; conversion plan; and recovery, contingency, and fallback plan.
- Index to related material.
- Service level agreement.

4.2.7 Deliverables to Be Produced from the Implementation Stage

The following deliverables should be produced by the end of the implementation stage:

- Full set of release and maintenance procedures.
- Detailed contingency, recovery, and fallback plan (if not already produced during the previous stage).
- Schedule and plan for the postimplementation review.
- Postimplementation review report.
- Signed letter of system approval.
- Detailed schedule for further postimplementation reviews.

- First reviews and verifications of the contents of the service level agreement.

4.2.8 Deliverables to Be Produced from the Maintenance Stage

The following deliverables should be produced during the maintenance stage of the system's life cycle:

- Detailed log of changes to the system.
- Copies of regular reviews and verifications of the service level agreement.
- Copies of regular postimplementation review reports.

5

MANAGING THE
PROJECT TEAM

A good worker is known by his tools.

Anonymous

The physical structure of the project is defined by the stages, tasks, and deliverables. In addition, the project has a personnel or staff structure defined by the various responsibilities within the project. The following checklists provide guidance for organizing these responsibilities. Later in the chapter, the recommended in-stage and end-stage project review points are defined in terms of the deliverables to be reviewed. This sets up a logical monitoring structure for the project and allows the project manager to achieve and demonstrate effective control of the project's progress. Finally, a description of the *types* of tools valuable to the project manager and the project team is provided.

An appendix to this chapter provides a representative set of current (1990/1991) proprietary tools available to the systems development project manager. With the speed of technological change today, this list will become outdated very quickly, but it does serve as an indicator of the range of tools "out there" for the project manager to choose from.

5.1 RESPONSIBILITIES FOR EACH LIFE CYCLE STAGE

The following chart provides an overview of the *management* and *deliverable* responsibilities across the system development life cycle.

Stage	Stage Management	Responsibility for Deliverables	
Feasibility study	Senior user	Senior systems manager	System description
			Project team organization
			Deliverables schedule
		Senior user manager	Business need
			Cost–benefit analysis
Requirements definition	Senior user	Senior user manager	Analysis of current system
			New system requirements
			Description of new system
			Estimates of next and subsequent stages
			Index to related material
System specification	Senior user	Senior user manager	System description
			Data requirements (shared with senior systems manager)
			Revised cost–benefit analysis
			Index to related material
		Senior systems manager	Data requirements (shared with senior user manager)
			Network and telecommunications requirements
			System controls
			Estimates of next and subsequent stages
System design	Senior systems manager	Senior systems manager	System summary
			Detailed system description
			Description of system controls
			Recommended design alternatives

(continued)

Stage	Stage Management		Responsibility for Deliverables

Stage	Stage Management		Responsibility for Deliverables
System test (*continued*)			Recommended program design techniques, standards
			Recommended implementation techniques
			Preliminary system test plan (shared with senior user manager)
			Estimates of next and subsequent stages
			Index to related material
		Senior user manager	Revised cost–benefit analysis
			Preliminary system test plan (shared with senior systems manager)
Program design and development	Senior systems manager	System project leader(s)	Detailed design system and program documents
			Detailed design system and program diagrams
			Detailed logic for each program
			Detailed documentation for each program
			Input–output descriptions
			Program source listings
			Control language (JCL) listings, if necessary
			System operators guides (shared with system operations)
			Results of unit tests
			Results of integration tests
		Senior systems manager	Estimate of next and subsequent stages, including implementation schedule, conversion, and contingency plans (shared with senior user

(*continued*)

Stage	Stage Management		Responsibility for Deliverables
Program design and development (*continued*)			manager, quality assurance, and operations) System test plan (shared with senior user manager and quality assurance) Index to related material
		Senior user manager	Estimate of next and subsequent stages (shared with senior systems manager, quality assurance, and operations) System test plan (shared with senior systems manager and quality assurance) User training and manuals User guide(s)
		Quality assurance	Estimate of next and subsequent stages (shared with senior user and senior systems managers and operations) System test plan (shared with senior systems and user managers)
		Operations management	Estimate of next and subsequent stages (shared with senior systems and user managers and quality assurance) Operators' training and manuals
System test	Senior systems manager	Senior systems manager, senior user manager,	Updated system test plan Full system test results Documentation of test results at variance with

(*continued*)

Stage	Stage Management		Responsibility for Deliverables
System test (*continued*)		and quality assurance	expected results and plans for resolution of these variances
		Senior user manager	Results of documentation tests
			Implementation schedule; conversion plan; recovery, contingency, and fallback plan
			Service level agreement
			Index to related material
Implementation	Senior user manager	Senior systems manager	Full release and maintenance procedures
		Senior user manager	Recovery, contingency, and fallback plans
			Schedule and plan for postimplementation review
			Post implementation review report
			Letter of system approval
			Schedule for further post implementation reviews
Maintenance	Senior user manager	Senior user manager	Log of changes to the system (shared with senior systems manager)
			Regular reviews of service level agreement
			Regular post implementation review reports

5.2 REVIEW POINTS FOR EACH LIFE CYCLE STAGE*

Each in-stage deliverable must be reviewed by the stage team and the stage manager. End-stage deliverables must be reviewed by the project management team, including at least the following:

*See the flow diagrams of stage activities in Chapter 3, where the required review points are shown diagrammatically.

- Senior user manager
- Senior systems manager
- Senior operations manager
- Quality assurance

5.2.1 Feasibility Stage

Only one review point is required in the feasibility stage. This is at the end of the stage when the feasibility study is presented to management.

5.2.2 Requirements Definition Stage

Review the following deliverables as they are produced:

- Scope of new system
- Analysis of the current system (if it exists)
- New system requirements
- List of tangible and intangible benefits
- Requirements definition document (end-stage document), including the prototype, if produced

5.2.3 System Specification Stage

Review the following deliverables as they are produced:

- Definition of type of system
- System schematic and system data dictionary
- Updated cost/benefit analysis
- System specification document (end-stage document)

5.2.4 System Design Stage

Review the following deliverables as they are produced:

- Overall system diagram
- Detailed system design for each alternative
- Updated cost/benefit analysis

- Evaluations of design alternatives
- System test plan for each alternative
- Documentation for users, operators, and training
- System design document (end-stage document)

5.2.5 Program Design and Development Stage

Review the following deliverables as they are produced:

- Work plan for stage
- Detailed design for each program
- Program code and unit test results for each program
- Integration test results
- Program design and development document (end-stage document)

5.2.6 System Test Stage

Review the following deliverables as they are produced:

- All system test results
- Implementation schedule
- Recovery, contingency, and fallback plans
- Service level agreement
- System test end-stage document

5.2.7 Implementation Stage

Review the following deliverables as they are produced:

- Release and maintenance procedures
- Schedule and plan for post implementation review
- Post implementation review report
- Schedule for further post implementation reviews
- Letter of system approval (end-stage document)

5.2.8 Maintenance Stage

Review the following deliverables as they are produced:

* Log of system changes (on a regular basis, at least monthly)
* Service level agreement reviews
* Post implementation review reports

5.3 SUGGESTED TOOLS FOR USE IN EACH STAGE

Many automated and mechanized tools are available to help the project manager effectively manage the system development life cycle. The following sections provide an indication of the *types* of tools recommended for each stage.

Feasibility Study

* Project request forms (see Chapter 3, the section on the feasibility study)
* Estimating tools (see Chapter 6)
* Payback schedule graphs (see reference 1)

Requirements Definition

* Ranking matrix technique (see reference 1)
* Walk-throughs (see reference 1)
* Data flow diagrams (see reference 1)
* Data dictionary
* Automated documentation

System Specification.   The same types of tools as in the requirements definition stage are recommended, plus the following:

* Structure charts (see reference 1)

System Design.   The same types of tools as in the system specification stage are recommended, plus the following:

- Structured design (see reference 1)
- CASE tools, if available and appropriate
- Object-oriented design and development tools (may be embedded in the CASE tool set)
- Project library (see reference 1)

Program Design and Development.   The same types of tools as in the system design stage are recommended, plus the following:

- Structured programming (if a procedural language is being used) (see reference 1)
- Automated test case generators

Also, Walkthroughs in this stage will be replaced by the more specific code inspections.

System Test.   The same types of tools as in the program design and development stage are recommended, plus the following:

- Cause–effect graphing

Implementation and Production.   All of the tools recommended in the preceding sections may be used, plus the following:

- Service level agreement
- Release procedures

5.4 LIFE CYCLE AND PROJECT MANAGEMENT TOOLS IN USE TODAY

The numbers and types of tools available for the systems development project manager increase each day within a bewildering explosion of claims and counterclaims by the various vendors. It is not easy to choose effective tools in this environment, but do not be discouraged. Many tools and techniques are available that can assist immeasurably in improving the productivity of the activities required to design, develop, install, and maintain application systems today.

The previous sections of this chapter included lists of *generic* tools to be used throughout the system development life cycle. These lists will not change greatly as time passes, because fundamental needs remain constant.

5.4.1 Complete System Development Life Cycle Methodologies

There are not a great number of software- or documentation-based packages that provide the user with a coherent, consistent set of techniques and tools for use *throughout* the system life cycle. Those that do so are often limited in their compatibility with evolving leading-edge design and programming technologies.

A few such "complete" methodologies are marketed and new ones are regularly added to the list. If you feel you really need one, be careful to choose one that fits *your* specific needs and about which you can obtain personal recommendations from known associates or organizations. Then be sure that you plan a trial that is not irrevocable.

The available "full life cycle" methodologies all represent a significant investment in time and resources in order to make them work in any specific environment. An essential approach to their implementation is to fully research the included life cycle to ensure its compatibility with your environment. Also, as with any proprietary package, detailed discussions with other users of the methodologies will be invaluable in determining how they work in practice. In addition, look for as much automation of the document-generation process as possible, as well as automation of the overall system generation procedures.

5.4.2 Project Management Tools

In addition to the preceding generic life cycle tools, a project management tool should be used to help manage the complete system development life cycle. This could be a simple paper-based, manual tracking system generated from the stage descriptions in this book, or it could be a fully automated project management system.

The best automated tools are those available on personal computers or workstations with full provision for pert charts, resource loading and leveling, subprojects, Gannt charts, and for planned, changed, and actual activities. Also, be sure that the tool you choose can handle the full amount of activities that you need to manage.

Whatever type of project **management** tool is used, it must be able to plan and track the following project parameters:

- Activities and tasks
- Deliverables
- Responsibilities
- Dates: start, finish, planned, actual, changed
- Human resources: groups, teams, individuals
- Material resources: hardware, software, facilities

The project management tool chosen must also have provision for adding narrative comments where necessary to complement the bare facts of the schedules, deliverables, and responsibilities.

Most available project management tools effectively provide a small subset of the functionality of the complete system development life cycle package. They help the project manager plan and track the project, but do not normally provide any help in analysis, specifications, design, programming, documenting, and testing. Project management tools are available on all sizes of machines, but the most ubiquitous and useful are those that run on PCs.

For large projects with many deliverables planned over a long period of time, these automated tools are very effective. But, in choosing such a tool the potential user must consider the amount of work required to input the various project parameters and the effort involved in updating schedules and events as the project progresses. For any project involving more than four or five full-time staff members and lasting longer than six months, it is probably worthwhile to use such a tool. It should be remembered that, in a multiple-project situation, to effectively utilize such an automated tool probably takes the full time of one person. So if one person is already planned to be 100% allocated to *manual* project planning and tracking, then the investment in an automated project management tool is justified. The single-project planner/tracker will then stand a chance of managing the growth in planning and tracking activities as the number of projects grows.

The available functionality and prices range from primitive task lists with end dates and single responsibilities for less than $100 to full definitions of tasks, subprojects, resource leveling, multiple predecessor, and successor dependencies, and more, for tens of thousands of dollars. As in buying a suit, choose the package that fits your needs, that you can afford, and that is justified within the overall project budgets. (Obviously, such a tool is more likely to pay for itself if used over a number of projects.)

5.4.3 CASE Tools

A new set of state of the art computer-assisted tools is becoming available to help the software developer. Computer-Aided Software Engineering (CASE) refers to any software-based tool that partially or fully automates some or all activities in the software development life cycle. Most of the popular tools are PC- or workstation-based, and some of the more effective ones are using the concepts of object-oriented programming. Databases, files, data, procedures, and even ready to use software modules are regarded as *objects* and manipulated via the workstation or PC into the overall system structure using graphical user interfaces. All objects to be manipulated are held in a *repository* for easy access. Once a comprehensive repository is built up, generating a new application can be achieved by simply calling up the required objects on the workstation screen and connecting them in a building-block approach to constructing programs and systems. This object-oriented programming is a new, friendlier, and more comprehensive and effective twist on the decades-old idea of reusable code.

If a suitable CASE tool exists for your environment, *use it*. But, use the free trial offers of temporary use that come with most reputable packages, talk to other users, and remember that you will need to have access to the source code if the package manufacturer goes out of business. Also, try to obtain a maintenance agreement.

Most available CASE tools use modern structured analysis, design, and programming techniques. If your organization already subscribes to a particular flavour of "structured" technique, it would be wise to pick a package that uses, or is compatible with, those specific tools. This will ease the acceptance of the CASE package by the existing systems staff.

CASE tools do not yet fully automate the complete systems development life cycle, and they are not all compatible, even within one manufacturer's tool kit. Therefore, the choice of such tools within an existing, sophisticated systems development operation must be carried out very carefully with regard to minimum disturbance of the current environment, unless the current practices *should* be eliminated.

A representative list of specific tools follows as an appendix to this chapter. Perhaps the best way to choose a suitable tool for your environment is to try a few, using the list in the appendix as a base, to talk to other users, and to develop your own, up to date statement of what *you* need in such a tool. Then be hard nosed about insisting on those requirements. You will probably find tools that fit your needs closely enough, but probably not at the first try. Also, remember that your systems folks are almost certainly doing some, if not most, things right. Choose tools that complement those good things in your environment. Don't throw the baby out with the bath water!

APPENDIX: TOOLS FOR THE PROJECT MANAGER*

Letters in parentheses (   ) following the name of each listed tool indicate the host hardware and/or software environment(s) that the tool is designed to operate in. These environments are designated as follows:

APL	Apollo
AT	AT&T
CDC	Control Data Corp
DEC	DEC (Digital Equipment, all systems)
DG	Data General
HP	Hewlett-Packard
HN	Honeywell
IM	IBM Mainframes, including minis
MA	Macintosh
NCR	NCR, Inc.
PC	IBM PC, PS/2, and compatibles
PRI	Prime Computer Systems
SUN	Sun Microsystems
UN	Unisys
UX	Unix
WA	Wang

There are many tools available in some categories, for example for project management and program construction. In general, the tools available only in the PC or Macintosh environment are much less expensive than those intended to work on mainframes. Choose a tool that fits your particular needs and budget and one that you can obtain first-hand recommendations about from organizations and people that you can trust.

*A list such as this becomes obsolete very quickly, so use it only as a guide to what is available. Also, as long as this list is, there are many more tools on the market.

Life Cycle Methodologies

These tool sets are applicable across the complete system development life cycle. They include project management facilities.

FIRSTCASE (IM, PC)	AGS Management Systems, King of Prussia, Pennsylvania
PRIDE (IM, PC)	M. Bryce & Associates, Inc., Palm Harbor, Florida
SPECTRUM (IM, PC)	Spectrum International, Culver City, California
TIP/PLAN/DEFINE (IM) (Combined with CASE 2000 tools, provides complete life cycle methodology)	NASTEC Corp., Southfield, Michigan

Project Management Tools (including Estimating Tools)

ACTION TRACKER (PC)	Information Research, Inc., Charlottesville, Virginia
ACUVISION (IM)	Systonetics, Fullerton, California
ADVANCED PRO-PATH 6 (PC)	SoftCorp, Inc., Clearwater, Florida
AMS TIME MACHINE (PC,HP)	Diversified Information Services, Inc., Studio City, California
APECS/8000 (DEC)	Automatic Data Processing, Ann Arbor, Michigan
ARTEMIS PROJECT (PC,IM,HP,UX)	Metier Management Systems, Houston, Texas
BARONET (PC)	Computerline, Inc., Pembroke, Massachusetts
CA-TELLAPLAN/ PLAN-MACS/ SUPER PROJECT	Computer Associates, Garden City, New York

EXPERT/ESTIMACS (IM,DEC,APL,SUN,PC)	
CAPITAL PROJECT MANAGEMENT SYSTEM (IM)	Data Design Associates, Sunnyvale, California
EASYTRAK (IM)	Cullinet Software, Westwood, Massachusetts
ESTIPLAN (PC)	AGS Management Systems, King of Prussia, Pennsylvania
FASTTRACK SCHEDULE (MA)	AEC Management Systems, Inc., Sterling, Virginia
HARVARD PROJECT MANAGER (PC)	Software Publishing Corp., Mountain View, California
INFORMATION MANAGER (MA)	AEC Management Systems, Inc., Sterling, Virginia
INSPECTOR (IM) (measures quality of COBOL programs)	Language Technology, Inc., Salem, Massachusetts
INSTAPLAN (PC)	Instaplan Corp., Mill Valley, California
LIFE CYCLE MANAGER (PC)	Nastec Corp., Southfield, Michigan
MAPPS (PC, IM, HP, WA, DEC, DG)	Mitchell Management Systems, Westborough, Massachusetts
MICROMAN II (PC)	Poc-It Management Systems, Santa Monica, California
MICRO PLANNER PLUS (PC,MA)	Micro Planning Software, San Francisco, California
MICROSOFT PROJECT (PC)	Microsoft Corporation, Redmond, Washington
MICROTRAK/PLOTTRAK (PC, UX, IM)	Softrak Systems, Salt Lake City, Utah
MI-PROJECT (IM)	Matterhorn, Inc., Minneapolis, Minnesota
MULTITRAK (IM, PC)	Multisystems, Cambridge, Massachusetts
N1100/N5500 (IM, PC, UN, DEC, WA, DG, HP, HN, PRI)	Nichols & Company, Culver City, California

OPEN PLAN/OPERA (PC)	Welcom Software Technology, Houston, Texas
PAC SERIES (PC, IM, DEC, WA)	AGS Management Systems, King of Prussia, Pennsylvania
PERTMASTER ADVANCED (PC)	Pertmaster International, Santa Clara, California
PEVA (PC)	Engineering Management Consultants, Troy, Michigan
PLANNER (DEC)	Productivity Solutions, Waltham, Massachusetts
PLANTRAC (PC, SUN, UX, APL)	ComputerLine, Inc., Pembroke, Massachusetts
PMS-80 ADVANCED (PC, UX)	Pinnell Engineering, Portland, Oregon
PMS-II (PC)	North America Mica, San Diego, California
PREMIS/PICOM (IM)	K&H Professional Management Services, Wayne, Pennsylvania
PRIMAVERA PROJECT PLANNER/PARADE (PC)	Primavera Systems, Bala Cynwyd, Pennsylvania
PROJECT/2 (IM, DEC)	Project Software & Development, Inc., Cambridge, Massachusetts
PROJECT ALERT (DEC, HP, APL)	CRI, Inc., Santa Clara, California
PROJECT BRIDGE (PC, WA)	Applied Business Technology, Inc., New York, New York
PROJECT-MANAGER (IM)	Manager Software Products, Lexington, Massachusetts
PROJECT OUTLOOK (PC)	Strategic Software Planning Corp., Cambridge, Massachusetts
PROJECT SCHEDULER 4 (PC, WA, HP, MA)	Scitor Corp., Foster City, California
PROJECT WORKBENCH (PC, WA)	Applied Business Technology, Inc., New York, New York
PROMIS (PC)	Strategic Software Planning

	Corp., Cambridge, Massachusetts
PROTHOS (PC, DEC, UX)	New Technology Association, Evansville, Indiana
PROTRACS (PC)	Applied Microsystems, Roswell, Georgia
QUICK-PLAN II (PC)	Mitchell Management Systems, Westborough, Massachusetts
QUICK SCHEDULE (PC)	Power Up, San Mateo, California
QWIKNET PROFESSIONAL (PC, DEC)	Project Software & Development, Inc., Cambridge, Massachusetts
SAS/OR (PC, IM, DEC, PRI)	SAS Institute, Cary, North Carolina
SCHEDULING & CONTROL (PC)	Softext Publishing Corp., New York, New York
SKYLINE (PC)	Applitech Software, Cambridge, Massachusetts
SURETRAK PROJECT SCHEDULER (PC)	Primavera System, Inc., Bala Cynwyd, Pennsylvania
SYNERGY (PC, DEC)	Bechtel Software, Acton, Massachusetts
TASK MONITOR (PC)	Monitor Software, Los Altos, California
TIMELINE (PC)	Symantec Corp., Novato, California
TOPDOWN PROJECT PLANNER	Ajida Technologies, Santa Rosa, California
TRAK (IM)	The Bridge, Inc., Millbrae, California
VAX SOFTWARE PROJECT MANAGER (DEC)	Digital Equipment Corp., Maynard, Massachusetts
VIEWPOINT (PC)	Computer Aided Management Inc., Petaluma, California
VIS1ON (DEC, PRI)	Systonetics, Fullerton, California
VIS1ONMICRO (PC)	Systonetics, Fullerton, California

VUE (PC, DEC, UX, HP, HN)	National Info Systems, Cupertino, California
WHO/WHAT/WHEN (PC)	Chronos Software, San Francisco, California
WINGS (PC)	AGS Management Systems, Inc., King of Prussia, Pennsylvania

CASE Tools

Business analysis and planning tools

AUTO-MATE PLUS (PC)	Learmonth & Burchett Management Systems, Houston, Texas
CASE TOOL SET (IM, DEC, DEC, UX) (includes data modeling)	Meta Systems, Ann Arbor, Michigan
DESIGN MANAGER (IM)	Manager Software Products, Lexington, Massachusetts
MANAGERVIEW (PC)	Manager Software Products, Lexington, Massachusetts
METHOD MANAGER (PC)	Manager Software Products, Lexington, Massachusetts
SPQR/20 (PC)	Software Productivity Research, Cambridge, Massachusetts

System Analysis Tools.   Many system analysis tools also provide system design and implementation support.

4FRONT STRATEGY (IM)	Holland Systems, Ann Arbor, Michigan
ABC FLOWCHARTER (PC)	Roycore, Inc., San Francisco, California
ANALYST/DESIGNER TOOLKIT (PC) (a full life cycle CASE tool)	Yourdon, Inc., Raleigh, North Carolina
ALLCLEAR (PC)	Clear Software, Brookline, Massachusetts

ANATOOL (MA)	Advanced Logical Software, Beverly Hills, California
CASE 2000 (PC, DEC)	NASTEC Corp., Southfield, Michigan
COMPUTER-AIDED REAL-TIME DESIGN TOOLS (DEC, UX)	Ready Systems, Sunnyvale, California
CONSOI (MA)	System OID, Inc., Saint-Foy, Quebec, Canada
CORVISION (DEC)	Cortex Corp., Waltham, Massachusetts
DEC VAXSET (DEC) (a full life cycle CASE toolset)	Digital Equipment Corp., Maynard, Massachusetts
DEFT (DEC,MA)	Deft Inc., Rexdale, Ontario, Canada
DESIGN/OA (MA,UX,PC)	Meta Software, Cambridge, Massachusetts
EXCELERATOR (PC,DEC)	Index Technology, Cambridge, Massachusetts
FOUNDATION (IM,PC) (a full life cycle analysis and design tool set)	Andersen Consulting, Chicago, Illinois
IEF (IM,PC,DEC,TAN,UX)	Texas Instruments, Plano, Texas
IEW/WS (PC,IM)	Knowledgeware, Atlanta, Georgia
LEVERAGE (PC,DEC)	DACOM, Manhattan Beach, California
PACBASE (IM, PC, UN) (analysis, design, and reverse engineering tool)	CGI Systems, Pearl River, New York
POSE (PC)	CSA, Inc., Woodcliff Lake, New Jersey
PROKIT ANALYST (PC)	McDonnell Douglas Information Systems, St. Louis, Missouri
STRUCTURED ARCHITECT (PC)	Meta Systems, Ann Arbor, Michigan
SYSTEM ARCHITECT (PC)	Popkin Software, New York, New York

TEAMWORK (DEC, UX, IM, PC)	Cadre Technologies, Providence, Rhode Island
THE DEVELOPER (PC)	Sterling Software, Naperville, Illinois
TURBOCASE (MA)	StructSoft, Inc., Bellevue, Washington
USER:EXPERT SYSTEMS (PC)	Information Engineering Systems, Dallas, Texas
VISIBLE ANALYST WORK-BENCH (PC)	Visible Systems Corporation, Newton, Massachusetts
VSDESIGNER (PC)	Visual Software, Santa Clara, California

System Design Tools

APPLAUD (PC)	International Consulting Enterprises Ltd., Chicago, Illinois
CASESTATION (DEC,UX)	Mentor Graphics, Beaverton, Oregon
CASEWORKS (PC)	Caseworks, Inc., Atlanta, Georgia
DESIGN (IM)	AdPac Corp., San Francisco, California
DESIGN/IDEF (MA)	Meta Software, Cambridge, Massachusetts
DFPD (IM)	AdPac Corp., San Francisco, California
IEF (IM)	Texas Instruments, Plano, Texas
LPS (IM,PC)	American Management Systems, Arlington, Virginia
MACDESIGNER (MA)	Excel Software, Marshalltown, Indiana
PERFORMANCE ARCHITEK (PC)	Wind Tunnel Software, Chicago, Illinois
POWERTOOLS (M)	Iconix, Santa Monica, California
PROCODE (PC) (system design, program construction, and reengineering)	Scandura Intelligent Systems, Narbeth, Pennsylvania

SOFTWARE BACKPLANE (DEC) (a CASE framework)	Atherton Technology, Sunnyvale, California
SOFTWARE THROUGH PICTURES (DEC,UX)	IDE, San Francisco, California
STRADIS (IM)	McDonnell Douglas Information Systems, St. Louis, Missouri
SYNON (IM)	Synon Inc., Larkspur, California

Database Modeling, Analysis, and Design Tools

BACHMAN DATABASE ADMINISTRATOR (IM) (a reengineering tool for DB2)	Bachman Info. Systems, Burlington, Massachusetts
BACHMAN RE-ENGINEERING PRODUCT SET (IM) (a database modeling, analysis, and design tool set)	Bachman Information Systems, Burlington, Massachusetts
ER MODELER/DESIGNER	Chen & Associates, Baton Rouge, Louisiana
IDEF/LEVERAGE & MODELPRO	D. Appleton Co. (DACOM), Manhattan Beach, California

Program Design and Construction Tools.   Many of the program design and construction tools provide testing guidelines and/or facilities.

ACCELL (UX)	Unify Corp., Sacramento, California
ACCENTR (DEC)	National Info Systems, San Jose, California
ADR/IDEAL (IM)	ADR, Inc., Princeton, New Jersey
ADS (IM)	Cullinet Software, Westwood, Massachusetts
AL-2000 (IM)	Genesys Software Systems, Methuen, Massachusetts
APPLICATION BUILDER (HP, DEC, DG, APL)	CRI, Inc., Santa Clara, California

APS DEVELOPMENT CENTER (IM, PC)	Sage Software, Rockville, Maryland
CA-UNIVERSE/ FLEXISCREEN (IM)	Computer Associates, Garden City, New York
CQS INFOTEC (IM)	Carleton Corp., Burlington, Massachusetts
CSP/AD (IM)	IBM Corp., Armonk, New York
CYGNET (IM)	Phoenix Software Co., Los Angeles, California
D THE DATA LANGUAGE (PC)	Caltex Software, Dallas, Texas
DATAFLEX (DEC, PC)	Data Access Corp., Miami, Florida
DYL/280 (IM)	Sterling Software, Chatsworth, California
ENTER/3270 (PC)	Aspen Research, Hillsborough, California
EXPRESS (IM)	Information Resources, Waltham, Massachusetts
FOCUS (IM, DEC, UX, WA, NCR, AT, APL)	Information Builders, New York, New York
FOCUS-UMF (IM)	Information Builders, New York, New York
GENER/OL (IM)	Pansophic Systems, Oak Brook, Illinois
IDEAL/ESCORT (PC)	ADR Inc., Princeton, New Jersey
IIS/DESTINY (DEC)	Intelligent Information Systems, New York, New York
INFO-DB (DEC)	Henco Software, Waltham, Massachusetts
INFORMIX-4GL (DEC, UX, PC)	Informix, Menlo Park, California
INGRES (DEC, UX, IM, PC)	Relational Technology, Alameda, California
INTELLECT (IM, DEC)	AI Corp., Waltham, Massachusetts
INTOUCH (PC, DEC)	Touch Technologies, San Diego, California

MAGNA (CDC)	Magna Software, New York, New York
MANTIS/MANTIS PC (IM, DEC, HN, PC)	Cincom Systems, Cincinnati, Ohio
MAPPER (UN, PC, UX)	Unisys, Blue Bell, Pennsylvania
MCR-QUERY SERIES (IM)	Michaels, Ross & Cole Ltd., Glen Ellyn, Illinois
MICROSTEP (PC)	Syscorp International, Austin, Texas
MILLENIUM:SDT (IM)	McCormack & Dodge, Natick, Massachusetts
MITROL (IM)	Mitrol, Inc., Woburn, Massachusetts
MODEL 204 (IM)	Computer Corporation of America Inc., Cambridge, Massachusetts
NATURAL (IM, DEC)	Software AG, Reston, Virginia
NATURAL ENGINEERING SERIES (DEC, IM, PC)	Software AG, Reston, Virginia
NETRON/CAP (IM, DEC, WA, PC)	Netron, Downsview, Ontario, Canada
NOMAD/PCNOMAD (IM, DEC, PC)	Must Software International, Norwalk, Connecticut
ORACLE (IM, DEC, UX, DG, AT, APL)	Oracle Corp., Belmont, California
PCEXPRESS (PC, AT)	Information Resources, Waltham, Massachusetts
PC-FOCUS (PC)	Information Builders, New York, New York
PC/HIBOL (IM, PC)	Matterhorn, Inc., Minneapolis, Minnesota
PDS-ADEPT (UN, UX, PC)	Parameter Driven Software, Inc., Birmingham, Michigan
POWERHOUSE/PC (DEC, HP, DG, PC)	Cognos, Inc., Peabody, Massachusetts
PRO-IV (IM, DEC, PRI, PC)	McDonnell Douglas, St. Louis, Missouri

PROGENI-GLE (UN)	Progeni Systems, Glendale, California
PROGRESS (PC, DEC, AT, UX, UN, SUN, HP)	Progress Software Corp., Bedford, Massachusetts
RAMIS (IM)	On-Line Software International, Fort Lee, New Jersey
SAS SYSTEMS (IM, DEC, PC, DG, PRI)	SAS Institute, Cary, North Carolina
SPEED II (WA)	TOM Software, Seattle, Washington
SSM/PROCOL (DEC, UX)	SSM, Inc., Montreal, Quebec, Canada
SYSTEM 1032 (DEC)	Compuserve Data Technologies, Cambridge, Massachusetts
TELON (IM, PC)	Pansophic Systems, Oak Brook, Illinois
TODAY (DEC, UX, PC, HP)	BBJ Computer Services, San Jose, California
TRANSFORM (IM)	Transform Logic Corp., Scottsdale, Arizona
UFO (IM)	On-Line Software International, Fort Lee, New Jersey
VAX RALLY (DEC)	Digital Equipment Corp., Maynard, Massachusetts
WWD CHARM (UX)	World Wide Data, New York, New York
ZFOUR (UX, WA, PC)	Business Computer Solutions, Inc., Miami, Florida

Reengineering Tools. Many reengineering tools provide testing guidelines and/or facilities.

ANALYZER (HP)	Aldon Computer, Oakland, California
ASTEC (IM, DEC, UX)	Advanced Systems Technology
AUDITEC (IM, PC)	Maintec, Inc., Honolulu, Hawaii

CA-TRANSIT/LIBRARIAN (IM)	Computer Associates, Garden City, New York
COBOL/GLOSSARY (IM)	MacKinney Systems, Springfield, Missouri
COBOL INTERFACE DOC (DEC, HON)	Softool Corp., Goleta, California
COBOL STRUCTURING FACILITY (IM)	IBM Corp., Armonk, New York
COBOL STRUCTURIZER (DEC, HON)	Softool Corp., Goleta, California
COBOL-TO-COBOL (IM)	Computer Task Group, Orchard Park, New York
COMPAREX (IM)	Sterling Systems Software, Rancho Cordova, California
DATA CORRELATION DOCUMENTATION SYSTEM/CSA (IM)	Marble Computer, Martinsburg, West Virginia
DATATEC (IM)	XA Systems Corp., Los Gatos, California
DATAXPERT (IM)	XA Systems Corp., Los Gatos, California
ENDEVOR-C1 (IM)	Legent Corp., Westborough, Massachusetts
HAWKEYE	Blackhawk Data Corp., Chicago, Illinois
INFORMATION GATHERING WORKBENCH (PC)	Knowledgeware, Atlanta, Georgia
NETRON/CAP DEVELOPMENT CENTER (IM, PC, DEC, WA)	Netron, Inc., Toronto, Canada
PATHVU/RETROFIT/REACT (IM, PC)	XA Systems Corp., Los Gatos, California
PM/SS (IM)	Adpac Corp., San Francisco, California
Q/AUDITOR (IM, WA, HP)	Eden Systems Corp., Carmel, Indiana
RECODER/INSPECTOR (IM)	Language Technology, Inc., Salem, Massachusetts

RECODER (IM)	Language Technology, Inc., Salem, Massachusetts
REFORMAT (IM, UN)	EDP Management, Inc., La Mesa, California
RE-SPEC (IM, PC, DEC, UX)	Software Products & Services, Inc., New York, New York
SMART (SUN, APL, UX)	Procase Corp., Santa Clara, California
STRUCT (IM)	Programmed Solutions, Marietta, Georgia
STRUCTURED RETROFIT (UX)	XA Systems Corp., Los Gatos, California
SUPERCASE (DEC)	Advanced Technology International
SUPERSTRUCTURE (IM)	Computer Data Systems
SYLVA FOUNDRY	Cadware, New Haven, Connecticut
TURNOVERPLUS (IM)	Conversions, Inc., Raleigh, North Carolina
VIA/INSIGHT/SMARTTEST (IM)	Viasoft Inc., Phoenix, Arizona
XPEDITER (IM)	Centura Software, Minneapolis, Minnesota

Testing Tools

COBOL PROGRAM ENVIRONMENT (DEC, HN)	Softool Corp., Goleta, California

System Configuration Tools

CCC (DEC, IM, UX, DG)	Softool Corp., Goleta, California

System Maintenance Tools

ABEND-AID (IM)	Compuware Corp., Farmington Hills, Michigan

CA-LIBRARIAN (IM)	Computer Associates, Garden City, New York
COBXREF (WA)	FWM Digitech, New York, New York
CROSS REFERENCE (IM)	Evansville DP, Evansville, Indiana
LOGICCHAIN (IM,UN)	Application Programming, Moorestown, New Jersey
PANVALET (IM)	Pansophic Systems, Oak Brook, Illinois
REMDOC (IM)	REM Associates, New York, New York
SYDOC (IM)	Syncsort, Woodcliff Lake, New Jersey
X-REF (IM)	National Database Software, West Bloomfield, Michigan

6

ESTIMATING

There is only one thing about which I am certain, and that is that there is very little about which one can be certain.

W. Somerset Maugham, *The Summing Up* (1938)
Doubleday & Co., Inc., New York, NY

Estimates are probably where the data processing folks get into the most trouble. It is a well-known fact of the DP world that systems development projects that come in under budget and on time are rarer than good low-cost systems programmers. Many of the discrepancies that occur between original estimates and the final costs and schedules are the result of inadequate specifications and designs. These inadequacies become exposed during the program design and development and system test stages, necessitating further design work and much additional programming and testing.

The best philosophical approach to estimating any systems development effort is to assume that these additional, unplanned efforts *will* be needed. Then ensure that sufficient controls are in place to recognize the need for rework as early in the systems development life cycle as possible. Additionally, it must be realized that an early, accurate estimate is impossible under these circumstances. Therefore, the estimate must be adjusted to fit the changes as they occur, and management must accept the inescapable fact that the first estimate may well be 100% in error! So, an estimate must be made at the start of the system development efforts and then subsequently at the end of each life cycle stage (as specified in Chapter 4). Management must commit in detail to the estimate for each stage to ensure adequate resources and in general to the changing, overall estimate for the complete project. We might call this creeping commitment or, more elegantly, *stage-limited commitment*.

There are a number of methods for estimating in this environment, ranging from rules of thumb to software-based algorithms. It must be realized, however, that none of these is foolproof and all are prone to significant errors. This will always be true as long as human interpretation of requirements and human programming activities are integral to the systems development life cycle.

6.1 ESTIMATING METHODS

Five generic estimating methods will be discussed in this chapter:

1. Using the life cycle resource distribution as a basis for calculation
2. Direct comparison of existing, completed projects with variance factors
3. Function points
4. Algorithms based on the estimated size of system
5. Software packages

Undoubtedly, there are and will be many other techniques and methods, but these five categories cover most of the variations that now can occur.

6.1.1 Using the Life Cycle Resource Distribution as a Basis

There is often a known distribution of costs (resources and time) of a project across the life cycle stages. This is obtained by direct experience from other projects or by the use of industry standards.

If we measure the resources used on the early stages of the life cycle of a particular project, we can then estimate the remainder of the project. In Figure 6.1, three man-months have been used in the first two stages, feasibility study and requirements definition. According to our expected resource distribution, based on our own or other relevant experience, this equates to 12% of the expected total. Therefore, at this stage we can estimate that the

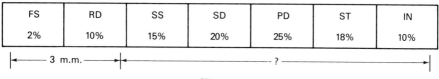

FS	RD	SS	SD	PD	ST	IN
2%	10%	15%	20%	25%	18%	10%

|← —— 3 m.m. —— →|← ——————————— ? ——————————— →|

25 m.m.

Figure 6.1   Estimating Using Life Cycle Resource Distribution

total project will take 25 man-months. Of course, this assumes that this project will have the same or similar characteristics as all the other projects being used in an information base.

6.1.2 Direct Comparison with Variance Factors

The previous example assumed an average project. Of course, there is no such thing. So we need to vary our base estimate, however it is arrived at, by some variance factors to take into account how different our project is from the average for our particular organization. The project parameters that can cause variances are size, complexity, number of users, and unknown factors.

- *Size:* If the proposed system is larger or smaller than the average, add or subtract the proportionate amount to or from the estimate. (Size of course is somewhat subjective, but usually relates to a "gut" feeling for the number of lines of code and the size and number of files or databases involved with the system. The function points method, discussed later in this chapter, provides a much more scientific approach to estimating size.)

- *Complexity:* If the proposed system is significantly more or less complex than the average, then add or subtract 20% to or from the base estimate. (Again, complexity is a largely subjective measure but can be gauged by the number of different files and databases being accessed and created and by the length of processed transactions, among other things.)

- *Users:* For each user organization other than the prime user involved with the project, add 5% to the base estimate.

- *Unknown factors:* If the project manager is dealing with unknown factors in any of the following major aspects of the project, then 20% should be added to the base estimate for each of the unknowns.

Operating software: If this will be the first time that the organization has used the operating system that the new system will run under, then this is an unknown factor.

Hardware: If this will be the first time that the proposed hardware configuration has been used in this organization, then this, too, is an unknown factor.

Project staff: If all the project staff, or the majority of them, are new to the organization, then this is probably the unknown factor that could have the most serious effect on the project's schedules and costs.

Figure 6.2 illustrates this technique, and Figure 6.3 shows how it could be applied in a real-life situation. In the example shown, the proposed system is 10% larger than the average and significantly more complex. In addition, three user organizations are involved, and there will be a new operating system, new hardware, and new project staff. Using the formula given, this project will take twice as many resources as the average.

6.1.3 Function Points Estimating

This estimating methodology was first proposed by Allan Albrecht of IBM in 1979 (reference 5). The measurement of the function points of a system is based on a formalized definition of its complexity and size.

Function points are a weighted sum of the different *types* of inputs, outputs, files, interfaces, and inquiries that a system processes. The system to be analyzed in this way could be a proposed or existing system.

```
"Average" Project Takes × Man-Months
• 10% larger, ADD 10%
• 10% smaller, SUBTRACT 10%
• Much more complex, ADD 20%
• Much less complex, SUBTRACT 20%
• ADD 5% for each additional user
• ADD 20% for each unknown of:
        • Operating System Software
        • Hardware
        • Project Staff
```

Figure 6.2 Estimating: Direct Comparison with Variance Factors

```
AVERAGE PROJECT TAKES 25 MAN-MONTHS
PROPOSED PROJECT:
    • 10% Larger                    + 10%
    • MUCH more complex             + 20%
    • 3 User orgs                   + 10%
    • NEW Operating System          + 20%
    • NEW Hardware                  + 20%
    • NEW Project Staff             + 20%
               TOTAL                + 100%
```

PROPOSED PROJECT ESTIMATE = 50 MAN-MONTHS

Figure 6.3 Estimating Example

Table 6.1 indicates how the function points value is arrived at for any given application system.

Albrecht provides a comprehensive set of guidelines to determine the level of complexity of each aspect of the system. Then the number of types of each entity listed in the table is multiplied by the appropriate factor, simple, average or complex, as shown. The total weighted sum is given the name of *total unadjusted function points (FC)*.

Processing Complexity. A processing complexity factor is then applied to the FC. This factor can cause as much as 35% to be added to or subtracted from the unadjusted function points value. This factor is calculated by estimating the effect on the complexity of the processing of the system of 14 separate characteristics. Each of these characteristics can have an effect measured from 0 to 5. If a given characteristic has no effect on the processing complexity of the system, then the measure is 0. On the other

TABLE 6.1 Function Count

Description	Complexity			Total
	Simple	Average	Complex	
External input types	×3	×4	×6	
External output types	×4	×5	×7	
Inquiry types	×3	×4	×6	
Master files and databases	×7	×10	×15	
External interfaces	×5	×7	×10	

Total *unadjusted* function points (FC) =

hand, a measure of 5 indicates a very strong effect on the processing complexity. These 14 measures are totaled, and their total is given the name of *total degree of influence (PC)*.

The 14 system characteristics are as follows:

Data communications	Performance
Heavily used configuration	Distributed functions
Transaction rate	On-line data entry
End-user efficiency	On-line update
Complex processing	Reusability
Installation ease	Operational ease
Multiple sites	Extensibility

The total degree of influence is then adjusted to arrive at an *adjusted processing complexity factor (PCA)*:

$$PCA = 0.65 + (0.01 \times PC)$$

As you can see, the value of PCA can vary from 0.65 to 1.35. Then the final function points measure is

$$FP = FC \times PCA$$

This function points value can be calculated for existing systems and a measure of "work-hours expended per function point" can be determined from the project records. This measure can be averaged for a given organization and then used as a basis for estimation of proposed system development projects.

Let's try an example. Table 6.2 represents a simple transaction pro-

TABLE 6.2 Function Count Table

	Complexity			
Description	Simple	Average	Complex	Total
External input types	×3	×4	×6	20
External output types	×4	×5	×7	61
Inquiry types	×3	×4	×6	28
Master files and databases	×7	×10	×15	22
External interfaces	×5	×7	×10	30
		Total *unadjusted* function points (FC) =		161

cessing system using a database approach with some on-line reporting requirements. There are five external input types of average complexity, ten simple external output types, and three complex external output types. Seven inquiry types of average complexity are required, and there are two master databases, one simple and one complex. Finally, there are three external system interfaces, one simple, one average, and one complex.

In terms of processing complexity, the 14 system characteristics for this simple system are designated as follows, using the 0 to 5 scores for each characteristic.

TABLE 6.3 Systems Characteristics Example

Data communications	3	Performance	2
Heavily used configuration	5	Distributed functions	1
Transaction rate	2	On-line data entry	5
End-user efficiency	4	On-line update	5
Complex processing	1	Reusability	3
Installation ease	5	Operational ease	5
Multiple sites	0	Extensibility	5
		Total PC =	46

The total adjusted degree of influence, PCA, is

$$0.65 + (0.01 \times 46) = 0.65 + 0.46 = 1.11$$

Then the total function points measure for this system (FP) is

$$FP = FC \times PCA = 161 \times 1.11 = 179 \text{ (approx.)}$$

Let's say that your systems development organization has developed a value of 0.3 function points per work-hour based on the function point values and the average work-hours expended on existing, completed projects. This simple new project is estimated to have a value of 179 function points. Therefore, the cost/resources estimate for the new project is 179 divided by 0.3, or 597 work-hours.

The effective use of this particular estimating method clearly requires religious recording of the time and resources expended on all system development activities.

It has been proved in practice that function points have a close correlation to work-hours expended and the eventual number of lines of code implemented. Also, a fairly accurate measure of function points can be arrived at early in the project, unlike more specific measures, such as lines of code.

Albrecht's complete methodology is described in reference 5.

6.1.4 Algorithms Based on Lines of Code

Many organizations and individuals have developed their own algorithms for estimating the resource expenditure of a system development project based on some estimate of the eventual size of the system. One such algorithm has been developed by Boehm (see reference 6). Boehm's algorithm deals only with the system design, program design and development, and system test stages. We can then use our earlier generalized resource distribution across the life cycle stages to extrapolate the estimate for the complete project.

This algorithm assumes an average project, so the variance factors discussed earlier could also be applied to the estimate. Size-related variances based on lines of code have, however, already been accounted for by the algorithm itself.

The algorithm used for this method is

$$\text{work-months} = 153.2 \times (\text{KLOC})^{1.05}$$

where KLOC = thousands of lines of code. The underlying assumption is that the actual programming language does not matter because a higher-level language will require fewer lines of code and therefore will result in a shorter development time.

Let's take an example. Suppose the size of a small system is estimated at 5000 lines of COBOL. Therefore, according to the formula, the resources expended during system design through system test will be

$$153.2 \times 5^{1.05} = 830 \text{ work-months.}$$

From our previous estimates of resources distribution across the system development life cycle, the period of system design through system test absorbs 63% of the total project resources. Therefore, the total project resource estimate is 1318 work-months.

Obviously, this formula is based on actual experience and takes into account all the ancillary work that goes on to fully install a system, from the first glint in a user's eye to the end of acceptance testing in the production environment. It includes the costs of all personnel involved during all stages of development. Nevertheless, this probably sounds excessive, so ensure that any formula or algorithm used fits your environment and reflects that environment's experience.

6.1.5 Software-based Estimating Tools

A number of tools are available to help the project manager develop a reliable estimate. Any good software development or project management package will have a set of estimating guidelines based on its own methodology.

Estiplan, a project management package from AGS Management, a subsidiary of NYNEX, contains detailed estimating guidelines, with some emphasis on the types of variance factors discussed earlier.

Two good software packages for estimating are the following:

1. ESTIMACS: Part of the Computer Associates, Inc., stable of products. This is a PC-based estimating software package. It requires a conversational session or sessions in which answers to a set of detailed questions about the proposed system are entered into the PC. It uses the function points method internally to arrive at its results.
2. PROMPT ESTIMATOR: This is also a microcomputer-based estimating package produced by Simpact Systems Ltd. in the United Kingdom. It is based on the PROMPT project management methodology marketed by Simpact Systems and is designed to be used with that package.

These are only examples. There are many others, and trade magazines such as *Infoweek, Software, Datamation,* and *ComputerWorld* regularly survey these tools. One of your best courses of action when choosing a package is to study several of these recent reviews and then try to talk to some current users to get a practical feel for how the tools will work in your specific environment.

The project management team intending to use any proprietary or academic estimating technique or product must be aware that any such tool will require customizing to fit the specific environment. One organization's work-hours per function point value will not be the same as another's, and no two organizations end up using exactly the same system development life cycle.

7

VARIATIONS ON A THEME OF A LIFE CYCLE

It is a bad plan that admits of no modification.

Publilius Syrus, *Moral Sayings,* 1st Century B.C.

So far in this book we have concentrated on the traditional system development life cycle. Increasingly in today's system development world, this traditional approach is not being used. There are six reasons for this.

1. Systems being developed directly by the end users
2. Prepackaged software
3. Use of fourth-generation languages, application generators, and CASE tools
4. Use of object-oriented program and system development
5. Prototyping
6. The organization has not yet even reached the stage of using the traditional life cycle

So, what changes occur in the life cycle because of these different ways of doing things? Let's examine the different situations, except for item 6, which we will ignore.

7.1 USER-DEVELOPED SOFTWARE

If the developers of the system are developing the software for their own use, for example, if the end-users are trained to use the system development equipment in order to design and code their own applications, then the system development life cycle could change.

The requirements definition and the system specification stages could be combined if business-oriented end users develop their own systems. This is because their definition of the system would not need to be translated into system-oriented language until the system design stage. Alternatively, it could be considered that the system design and system specification stages are combined. These changes are possible because, with these particular users developing their own systems, the translation from business to technical language will not be such a major step.

Life Cycle for Systems Developed by Business Users

Feasibility study	Combined requirements definition and system specification	System design	Program design and development	System test	Implementation and maintenance

or

Feasibility study	Requirements definition	Combined system specification and system design	Program design and development	System test	Implementation and maintenance

If the end users are themselves systems professionals or engineers, then the systems they develop for themselves can use yet another variation on the traditional life cycle. In this case, it is likely that these worthy folk will jump straight into system design after having carried out a perfunctory feasibility study. This may not necessarily be the best way to develop such systems, but it will be almost impossible to persuade these professionals to bother with requirements definitions and system specifications. If these developers agree to support their own systems, then so be it. The life cycle tasks and checkpoints defined in Chapters 4 and 5 will assure the integrity of the system to a large extent.

Life Cycle for Systems Developed by Systems
Professionals or Engineers

Feasibility study	System design	Program design and development	System test	Implementation and maintenance

Other tools and techniques available today will almost certainly be used by systems professionals and end users to speed up and simplify the system development process. In these cases, the potential shortening of the life cycle detailed previously will be further assisted by the new tools. The effect of these tools is discussed in the next sections.

7.2 PREPACKAGED SOFTWARE

Many application programs and even some full-fledged systems can be fully implemented by using ready-made software. The software industry has grown enormously over the last two or three decades, and most software development managers must consider the "make versus buy" question before embarking on a costly, difficult, and risky internal software development journey.

In the best (but unfortunately rare) cases, a package can be found that not only implements all the required functionality, but also fits perfectly into the existing software and hardware environment. In this happy situation, most of the system design stage and all of the program design and development stage can be eliminated. In addition, the system test stage will be significantly shortened, and *if* the purchased package is exceptionally well defined and documented, the system specification stage could also be virtually ignored or simply combined with the requirements definition stage. Therefore, in this ideal case, the system development life cycle would look as follows:

Life Cycle Using "Perfect" Software Packages

Feasibility study	Requirements definition (including system specification)	System test	Implementation and maintenance

In more realistic cases, the software package or packages will not fill all the needs of the proposed system and will not be perfectly documented. Therefore, the more likely version of the life cycle will require some design and development of those required functions that are not included. The requirements definition and system specification stages can still probably be combined, as the system development manager's responsibility is to ensure that any purchased package must be well documented. So, in this more practical case, the life cycle will be as follows:

Practical Life Cycle Using Software Packages

Feasibility study	Requirements definition (including system specification)	System design and program design and development	System test	Implementation and maintenance

7.3 FOURTH-GENERATION LANGUAGES, APPLICATION GENERATORS, AND CASE TOOLS

The aim of fourth-generation languages (4GLs) is to enable a direct translation from user requirements into a programming language. Therefore, instead of the programs being written in procedural languages such as COBOL, FORTRAN, Pascal, and Ada, the user would use a nonprocedural, human-oriented language to describe the required system functions. This language would be the 4GL that the computer can understand directly. If such languages were generally available, there would be little need for the system specification, system design, and program design and development stages in the life cycle. Detailing the full set of system requirements in the 4GL would, in effect, "write" the complete system. All that would be left would be the need to fully test the system and install it.

The life cycle in this situation would then be as follows:

Life Cycle Using a "Perfect" 4GL

Feasibility study	Requirements definition	System test	Implementation and maintenance

It is more likely that the 4GL is not as human-oriented as the above description suggests. Most probably it will be somewhat procedural and will require that a small amount of system design be carried out. Also, most of the available 4GLs are limited in their functionality, and a full system will require that some of its functions be implemented via procedural languages, necessitating some small amount of program design and development. So the realistic life cycle for using a 4GL is more like the following:

Practical Life Cycle Using a 4GL

Feasibility study	Requirements definition	System design and program development (minimal)	System test	Implementation and maintenance

Application generators have similar objectives to those of 4GLs. They consist of techniques, usually PC-based, that allow a system designer to define system requirements in user-oriented terms. These requirements are then taken by the automated application generator and translated into system components, that is, program modules. The effect on the life cycle of application generators, "perfect" or otherwise, is similar to that of 4GLs.

CASE tools, in this context, can be considered to be a selected set of tools that will effectively act as a coordinated set of 4GLs, application generators, and more tools to automate much of the systems development life cycle. The impact of the better ones is similar to that of the "perfect" 4GLs and application generators described previously.

7.4 OBJECT-ORIENTED PROGRAMMING

Object-oriented system development treats the activity of developing software systems as one of manipulating *objects*. The manipulated objects can be combinations of precoded modules or programs, data records, files or databases, and automated procedures of all kinds along with codified processing and procedural rules. These objects are stored in an interconnected set of libraries and databases known as an object class library or an object *repository*. Any process requiring the use of any of the stored objects to build a system simply needs to access them, copy them, perhaps modify them, and add them via some predefined interconnections to the growing system. Modified objects will become new objects and be added to the library or repository. When the completed system runs, it calls or accesses the *system* objects, carries out the required manipulation(s), and returns them to the system libraries or databases, perhaps creating some new system objects at the same time. With today's sophisticated and user-friendly micro-computers and desk workstations, object manipulation can be carried out using the graphic and icon-based screen interfaces.

Object-oriented system development is a significant enhancement of the old ideas of reusable code and structured programming and as such has a significant impact on the system development life cycle similar to that of "perfect" 4GLs and application generators. If all objects needed in a system were already existing in the object library, this technique would indeed act like the "perfect" 4GL on the system development life cycle. Additionally, the system developed would be much more reliable and much easier to maintain and update than traditionally designed systems.

7.5 PROTOTYPING

Prototyping, or heuristic development, as it is often called, consists of producing a reduced function version of the proposed system in a very much shortened time frame and at much reduced costs compared with what would be expected from normal system development activity. This version of the system can then be used by the developers and the users to check out their assumptions and the practicability of the design.

Frequently, several successive prototypes are built, each using the previous prototype as a starting point and becoming progressively more sophisticated and complete, until the point is reached when the user is satisfied that the latest prototype is actually complete enough to serve as the production system.

This type of development forces a high degree of user involvement with the result that the system design problems are inevitably dealt with early in the life cycle. In addition, the system is developed faster and the final product is much more bug free than those developed by traditional methods.

The life cycle does not change because of the use of prototypes, but it is often repeated in rapid cycles. The programming languages and hardware and software environment may change as the prototypes become closer to the production version. The first prototype may be produced in BASIC or Pascal on a personal computer as part of the requirements definition stage, and the final production version may, because of production volumes, be implemented in C on an IBM mainframe under MVS/XA or UNIX.

The iterative development style encouraged by the prototyping technique is ideally suited to the top-down design and development employed by most of the design techniques already mentioned. Each successive prototype can implement deeper levels of the system hierarchical structure until the whole system exists. This also means that the system development staff must themselves be more skilled in all parts of the life cycle.

7.5.1 Separate Prototypes

There are two main types of prototyping. Separate prototyping means that each successive prototype is effectively thrown away, except for the last one, which is converted into production. Each prototype is subjected to a suitable version of the full life cycle, but the early stages are carried out successively much more quickly because of the learning process that goes on. Also, the latter stages involved with conversion and implementation can be omitted from some of the early prototypes. Each prototype can be started before the previous is completed, so there will be some overlapping of activities as shown in Figure 7.1. This type of prototyping is used when the full requirements of the system simply cannot be met by the environment of the early prototypes.

7.5.2 Prototyping by Successive Development

This type of prototyping is becoming more popular because it is faster and because the user-friendly environments that are conducive to early prototypes are becoming more powerful in terms of the larger applications that they can handle. The only real difference between this and the separate prototype technique is that here separate prototypes are not discarded but are used as the basis for the next one. Very often, in the real world, the user is

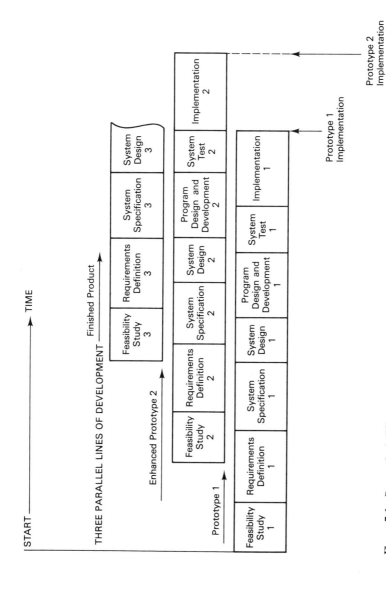

Figure 7.1 Prototyping's Effect on the Life Cycle

increasingly accepting one of the early prototypes as being "good enough" for the production system.

7.5.3 Modifications to the Life Cycle Caused by Prototyping

By using prototyping, the system development life cycle will become shortened, particularly in the program design and development and system testing stages. In addition, it may be possible to merge the system specification and system design stages because of the close working relationship of the users and the DP staff generated by the joint creation of the first prototype in the requirements definition stage.

7.5.4 Prototyping Tools

All system development tools can be used during the development of protoypes, but it is best to use some of the more state of the art tools, such as fourth-generation languages, query languages and application generators, and object-oriented development. The use of an application generator along with the prototyping technique is one of the more powerful approaches to system development. In such cases, the first prototype often becomes the production version of the system.

All the previous modifications to the system development life cycle are possible using the tools identified. But, even with all these apparent reductions in the time required to develop systems, all the tasks and deliverables defined as necessary in the traditional life cycle are still needed. The difference is that, with these state of the art tools and techniques, many of the tasks and deliverables are automated. But, they are still there!

8

THE FUTURE OF PROJECT MANAGEMENT

The Future isn't what it used to be.

Anonymous

For years, the imminent demise of programming as a profession has been rumored. Like Mark Twain's premature death, these rumors have been and still are greatly exaggerated. Similarly, with the advent of the state of the art project management and system development tools mentioned in the previous chapters, and many more appearing each day, many systems developers believe that project management can be virtually ignored because of the speed with which future systems will be developed. They are wrong, of course, just as those who still believe programmers are a dying breed are wrong.

As the techniques of systems development change, so will the techniques used to manage the systems development projects. The previous chapter on the variations in the systems development life cycle illustrated how the new development techniques affect the life cycle. As shown there, although the development process will very definitely be enhanced and accelerated, there will always be significant work to be done, involving different disciplines and many tasks and deliverables. Also, the potential use of computers in business and in our personal lives has only just begun. The number and size of applications automated in the future will far surpass those developed up to now. Even with perfectly functioning, user-friendly applications generators, management of the systems development activities will be more important than ever. In fact, as the software development discipline matures, more and more traditional, bottom-line-oriented measures will be applied to the production of software. This will of necessity impose strong management controls.

What differences will there be, if any, between the future project management methods and what we do today? There will be an evolution of techniques, much as is going on right now in the techniques of system design and programming. This evolution will lead, sooner or later, to some significant changes. The following is a brief list of potential areas of change:

- Combination of graphic and voice-oriented user interfaces with object-oriented development that will compress the early life cycle stages into one single design and implementation stage.
- Automated recording of deliverables linked to the project management system, thereby providing automated progress updates and reports.
- Automated, electronic-mail messages or warnings to significant project members detailing completed or about-to-be missed deliverables.
- Continually updated estimates of the remainder of the project as progress is recorded and changes are made.
- Documentation generated as part of the design and development process (this will probably be delivered as a function of application generators).
- Test conditions and scenarios developed automatically as part of the system development process.
- Extension of the automated project management process into the operational life of the system.

Prerequisite to these improvements in project management is the comprehensive use of a consistent set of system development life cycle methodologies and modern system design and development techniques, such as the family of structured techniques and the new idea of object-oriented programming.

With these techniques accepted as a way of life in systems development, the management of the systems projects will become easier and more procedural, especially as assisted by PC- or workstation-based project management software. All effective project management will be achieved with extensive software assistance.

Project management, as with all systems-development-related activities, will be carried out with user-friendly software packages running mostly on PCs and workstations. Most of the routine reporting will be automatically generated, so the human interface will be able to concentrate on changes to schedules and specifications and similar data input, ideally on an on-line basis. Therefore, even with all the state of the art changes to software development and project management, the task of project management will remain as important as it is today, and probably even more so.

REFERENCES

1. David King, *Current Practices in Software Development,* Prentice Hall, Englewood Cliffs, NJ, 1984.
2. Philip Crosby, *Quality Is Free,* Mentor Press, New American Library, New York, NY, 1979.
3. Robert Block, *The Politics of Projects,* Yourdon Press, Prentice Hall, Englewood Cliffs, NJ, 1983.
4. Frederick P. Brooks, *The Mythical Man-Month,* Addison-Wesley, Reading, MA, 1975.
5. Allan Albrecht, "Estimating Using Function Points," *IEEE Transactions on Software Engineering,* November 1983, Volume SE-9, No. 6, pp. 639–648.
6. Barry Boehm, *Software Engineering Economics,* Prentice Hall, Englewood Cliffs, NJ, 1981.

INDEX

A

Application generators 2, 3, 6, 33, 94, 97, 98, 100, 102, 101, 104
Application(s) software/system 1, 2, 7, 8, 9, 10, 19, 22, 66, 88, 95, 96, 103
Audit (DP auditors) 12, 20, 51

B

Brooks, Fred 6

C

CASE (Computer-Assisted/Aided Software Engineering) 3, 66, 69, 94, 97
Change control 13, 39

Commitment—stage-limited (creeping) 18, 20, 21, 86
Configuration management 22
  hardware 88
  testing 35
Contingency/recovery/fallback plan 34, 36, 49, 50, 51, 55, 56, 60, 61, 64
Conversion plan 34, 36, 55, 56, 60, 61
Cost/benefit analysis 21, 25, 29, 30, 32, 44, 46, 53, 54, 55, 59, 60, 63, 64
Costs (project) 1, 3, 6, 8, 9, 15, 18, 20, 29, 37, 42, 43, 44, 46, 48, 51, 53, 85, 86, 88, 91, 92, 99
Crosby, Philip 7

D

Data dictionary 30, 31, 32, 44, 45, 55, 63, 65
Data flow diagrams (DFDs) 30, 54, 65